Malice in Blunderland

Malice in Blunderland

by
Thomas L. Martin, Jr.

McGraw-Hill Book Company
New York   St. Louis   San Francisco
Düsseldorf   London   Mexico
Sydney   Toronto

72267

123456789 BPBP 79876543

Library of Congress Cataloging in Publication Data

Martin, Thomas Lyle.
  Malice in Blunderland.

  1. Management—Anecdotes, facetiae, satire, etc.
I. Title.
PN6231.M2M3   658.4′002′07   73–4376
ISBN 0–07–040617–0

Excerpts from pp. 69, 77, 89, 95, and 113–114 of *The House of Intellect* by Jacques Barzun: Copyright © 1959 by Jacques Barzun. By permission of Harper & Row, Publishers, Inc. (References 57, 76, 82, and 83.)

Material on page 83 adapted from the October 1970 issue of *College Management* Magazine is from the article "What Does the Dean Do?" by Dean John Randolph Willis, pp. 26–27. This article is copyrighted © 1970 by CCM Professional Magazines, Inc. All rights reserved.

Preface

If you want to be a carpenter, plumber, or mechanic, there are dozens of books available to tell you how to do it. If you want to be a lawyer, engineer, doctor, accountant, computer programer, or admiral, there are schools you can go to that will instruct you in the appropriate arts and sciences. And so it goes for every field of human endeavor—farmer, embalmer, optician, or astrologer—books and schools are always available to the interested learner.

But for someone who aspires to be a bureaucrat, such resources are simply not sufficient. It is true that in recent years there has been a spate of books examining various facets of the executive problem. The works of C. Northcote Parkinson, Laurence J. Peter and Antony Jay immediately come to mind. These have been important contributions to understanding why the corporate bureaucracy becomes a wonderland of blunders, a veritable blunderland of mishap, delay, confusion, maladroitness, and induced group paranoia. These authors provide valuable insights, but all suffer from the attempt to make their laws, principle, or analog all encompassing—each attempts to create a cosmology for organizational behavior. The works of many lesser contributors tend to suffer from this same defect. These attempts to achieve universality are doomed to failure because the extensive variety of bureaucracies and the many aspects of human response to them lead to an incredible diversity of situations that cannot be described accurately by a few highly generalized laws or principles.

The world of contemporary bureaucracies is far too rich a

vein of human foible to yield wholly to such simplistic approaches. Blunderland is a complex world, at least as complicated as high energy physics, and therefore requires an equally extensive collection of laws and principles for its description. Thus, the aim of this book is to assemble in one place, in related sequences, all of the laws of organizational and bureaucratic behavior that can be found.

I have lived in or with bureaucracies all my life. I know that many of the "good things" of life that we take for granted are often the result of bureaucratic effort. I also know that bureaucrats and bureaucracies are the architects of much of the mischief, or the malice, intentional or unintentional, that characterizes the world today. Thus, the fundamental assumption undergirding this book is that the bureaus and the bureaucrats are the essential causes of the malice prevalent in blunderland.

Unlike other books treating special aspects of the general subject, proofs of laws and principles are not offered here. Each law, principle, rubric, or effect is taken to be so self-evident that extensive documentation is not required.

It has been necessary to take substantial liberties with real time and actual events, and I have been very free in presenting as laws, principles, and rubrics the observations of others. The authors of many of these statements will recognize their own words to be sure, but they would be quite surprised to find them identified as laws or principles. But the fact that they failed to understand the importance of their own words and their application to bureaucratic behavior is scarcely reason for us not to honor them.

I am indebted to many people for their contributions to this effort. They are mostly all identified appropriately in the Sources and References section at the end of the book. However, I do want to say particular thanks to Mike O'Hagan and Bob Saunders for their special encouragement and help. I also appreciate the help of Arthur A. Collins and W. L. Everitt, who both advised me to make a major change in an early draft (failure to make this change would have been a dreadful blunder). Editorial assistance from Frances Curtis is acknowledged with profound gratitude. Finally, the work on this book began in a hospital bed and got this far only because of the unflagging support and constructive assistance of my wife. Thanks, Tootie.

THOMAS L. MARTIN, JR.
Dallas, Texas

Contents

Malice in Blunderland

chapter one

Kludgemanship

Recently I bought a new car for my wife. The choice was entirely hers; I told her she could have whatever she wanted—price was not a consideration. Luckily, or so it seemed, the one she picked was well engineered and appeared to be carefully manufactured, with no evidence of shoddy material or slipshod workmanship.

This illusion was short lived. Shortly after driving away from the dealer's show room, my wife found it necessary to make a left turn. As she turned the steering wheel the emergency signal light control, located on the steering column, released, and *all lights,* fore and aft, commenced flashing. It soon became evident that this happened every time the steering wheel was turned by more than about twenty degrees in any direction.

We returned immediately to the dealer's service department confident that this minor problem would soon be remedied. Our "service consultant"—it's what they call "sweetheart service"—assured us that the problem was trivial, easily correctible in a few minutes if we cared to wait, and we should soon be on our way, deliriously happy with our new car. We decided to take his advice and wait.

The car was moved to the shop area and a "skilled, factory-trained mechanic" disassembled the steering column to determine the source of the difficulty with the control of the emergency signal light flasher. This proved to be a very simple operation because of the excellent engineering supporting the design of the vehicle. Unfortunately, in the process of disassembling the steering column, the mechanic dropped a raceway, which is a little gizmo that keeps ball bearings in the proper position. It is the function of these particular bearings to keep the steering wheel securely centered. When the raceway was dropped, one of the tiny, but absolutely essential, ball bearings was lost in the ensuing confusion, and the steering column could not be reassembled. A replacement bearing was not in stock, naturally—not by the dealer, not by the regional distributor, not, [as it subsequently developed] several days later, by anyone in the United States. It had to be ordered from Germany, and it took the manufacturer, presumably the little elves in the Black Forest, something over two weeks to locate a spare. During this entire period the car sat immobile in the dealer's shop. Of necessity and naturally, my wife took my car while I bummed rides from friends and associates, straining many personal relationships quite severely.

Finally, the replacement part arrived. It was delivered to Texas to be sure—not to Dallas, where we live, but to El Paso, which is more than 600 miles away. It took three days of increasingly angry telephone calls to discover this, combined with a number of tense confrontations with the service manager. Greyhound Express eventually got the part to our dealer in Dallas, and the steering column was reassembled.

An unnecessarily cheerful "service consultant" called to say that the car was ready. We went to get it, our anger over the long delay tempered by relief that the problem and the inconvenience were over at last.

We drove the car away and—that's right—the emergency flasher was defective, just as before, releasing every time the steering wheel was turned. But that wasn't all. None of the signal lights worked, and the steering wheel was twisted ninety degrees to the right when the front wheels were pointed straight ahead—and the horn steadfastly refused to make a sound.

A story such as that ought to be funny, but it isn't because it is so commonplace. Things that happen everyday are not funny. Only unusual things are funny, and there is nothing unusual today about mishap, confusion, delay, and mistake.

Today, things just never seem to go quite right: organizations are unresponsive, equipment fails, plans go awry, computers make mistakes, well-intentioned people foul up—a *glitch* always appears. The glitch was first discovered by engineers in the early stages of the space program. However, it soon became evident that glitches are very common in all human activity. This led to the following general definition of a glitch.

The Glitch Defined

An inherent, built-in, organic fallibility in a design or a plan or an equipment or in any human contrivance.

Glitches occur even under the best of circumstances, even when matters are not being helped along by the natural human propensity to screw things up.

James Clerk Maxwell, one of the greatest scientists in history, whose discoveries made radio possible, jokingly postulated the existence of invisible demons to account for otherwise inexplicable effects, or to account for an otherwise unprovable assumption in a theory. These Maxwell demons were widely invoked to account for the otherwise unaccountable. About the time of World War II they were replaced by the more popular and more general gremlin concept which was necessary to explain the dramatic increase in the number and kinds of things going wrong with equipment and plans during the war years.

The gremlins were conceived to be invisible creatures who acted capriciously, maliciously, and in the most unexpected ways. But perceptive and astute observers discovered that glitches did not occur in wholly capricious ways. Rather, it was found that there is a fundamental *predictability* of things going wrong. As with all scientific insights, efforts were made to describe this phenomenon in terms of a general principle or law. If such a law could be developed and stated, then it could be subjected to carefully controlled scientific experiments designed to test the range of validity. Moreover, if such a law could be established, it would disprove the Gremlin Theory.

The earliest attempt to formulate a general law to explain the occurrences of glitches is of unknown date, but it is believed to be due to Murphy. His findings were embodied in three laws of great generality.

Murphy's Laws*

First Law—*If something can go wrong, it will.*

Second Law—*When left to themselves, things always go from bad to worse.*

Third Law—*Nature always sides with the hidden flaw.*[1]

These laws have stood the test of time and events and are now fully accepted as part of contemporary conventional wisdom. Each of us, in the daily process of living, sees experimental confirmation of these laws. As a result, the naive belief in capricious gremlins has largely disappeared.

Murphy's First Law has been so universally experienced and so generally published that it exists in a number of slightly different forms. One refinement that seems especially good appeared in 1972 as follows:

Revision of Murphy's First Law

If anything can go wrong (with a mechanical system), it will, and generally at the moment the system becomes indispensable.[120]

In addition to the different versions of the law itself, a large number of corollaries have been postulated to account for highly special cases. The following list is comprehensive but far from complete.

Corollaries to Murphy's First Law

It is impossible to make anything foolproof because fools are so ingenious.

Any wire or tube cut to length will be too short.

Interchangeable parts won't.

Identical units tested under identical conditions will not perform identically in the field.

After any machine or unit has been completely assembled, extra components will be found on the bench.

Components that must not and cannot be assembled improperly, will be.

All constants are variables.

In any given computation, the figure that is most obviously correct will be the source of error.

The probability of a dimension being omitted from a set of instructions is directly proportional to its importance.

After the last sixteen mounting screws are removed from an access plate, it will be discovered that the wrong access plate has been removed.[120]

There are literally millions of Murphys, of course, and it is desirable to give appropriate credit where it is due for what has proven to be a monumental contribution to man's understanding of nature. No one knows for sure, but there is good reason to believe that his first name was Edsel.

Edsel Murphy had a close friend named Finagle who had gained early fame with the discovery of the *Finagle Factor*. The Finagle Factor allows one to bring *actual* results into immediate agreement with *desired* results easily and without the necessity of having to repeat messy experiments, calculations, or designs. It was instantly and immensely popular with engineers and scientists, but found its greatest use in statistics and in the social sciences where actual results so often greatly differ from those desired by the investigator. The Finagle Factor is commonly credited with being the single most important element in the emergence of the social sciences to their present status. Indeed, it is generally felt that the Finagle Factor is to the social sciences what Einstein's Theory of Special Relativity is to physics. We will now review the elements of the Finagle Theory of Special Relativity:

The Finagle Factor is essentially, and inescapably, a tool of the dealer in paper work. Actual results, as reported on paper —probably with a computer intermediary—can, with the Finagle Factor, be adjusted with great convenience to produce desired results. Thus:

$$\begin{pmatrix} \text{Desired results} \\ \text{on paper} \end{pmatrix} = \begin{pmatrix} \text{Finagle} \\ \text{Factor} \end{pmatrix} \times \begin{pmatrix} \text{Actual} \\ \text{results} \end{pmatrix}$$

It is obvious that the entire process is a stimulating exercise for liberal intellectuals, particularly those in government who work with the budget.

Eventually, however, the desired results on paper must be transformed into the desired results *in fact*. This leads, always and without fail, to the production of a *kludge* (pronounced kloodj). In other words:

$$\begin{pmatrix} \text{Desired results} \\ \text{in fact} \end{pmatrix} = (\text{Kludge}) \times \begin{pmatrix} \text{Desired results} \\ \text{on paper} \end{pmatrix}$$

Fundamentally, a kludge is a means, a plan, a scheme, or a device arranged to accommodate a Finagle. That is, the Finagle Factor corrects numerical or mathematical errors while the kludge is the practical method of physically implementing the Finagle. The intrinsic character of the kludge was misunderstood for many years until it was defined formally and precisely by Granholm.

Granholm's Definition of the Kludge

An ill-assorted collection of poorly matching parts forming a distressing whole.[111]

One of the most important results in the Finagle Theory of Special Relativity is achieved by combining the two previous equations, the one which defines the Finagle Factor and the other which defines the kludge. This leads to the following result.

$$\begin{pmatrix} \text{Desired results} \\ \text{in fact} \end{pmatrix} = (\text{Kludge}) \times \begin{pmatrix} \text{Finagle} \\ \text{Factor} \end{pmatrix} \times \begin{pmatrix} \text{Actual} \\ \text{results} \end{pmatrix}$$

This is *the* basic equation undergirding the entire theory of Finagle Relativity and the practice of kludgemanship.

A very interesting result is achieved by taking the ratio of the desired results in fact to the actual results. Thus:

$$\frac{\text{Desired results in fact}}{\text{Actual results}} = (\text{Kludge}) \times (\text{Finagle Factor})$$

It is immediately apparent that the "results" appearing in both the numerator and denominator on the left cancel. This is in accordance with the rules of algebra. More important, the fact that "results" cancel out is a predictable result from the practice of advanced kludgemanship. This suggests that the product of a kludge and a Finagle Factor is a dimensionless constant which universally cancels results. Indeed, Martin has speculated that this product may be one of Nature's few fundamental constants. Be that as it may, nearly everyone agrees that the product of one kludge and one Finagle Factor invariably equals one SNAFU—Situation Normal, All Fouled Up.

It is often jokingly said that a camel is nothing more than a horse designed by a committee. And it is true that design always involves many resolutions of conflicting objectives. When these resolutions are sought through committee consensus, kludges generally result. And a camel certainly appears to be a biological kludge—an ill-assorted collection of poorly matching parts forming a distressing whole.

Kludges are commonly found in manufactured products, frequently through efforts to reconcile conflicting design constraints. For example, in the middle 1930s Chrysler introduced a new model car called the Airflow. It attempted to apply streamlining principles to the car body while maintaining adequate head, leg, and trunk room. The resulting car looked like a gargantuan pregnant Volkswagen. Of course, this was at a time when automobiles were still designed for ordinary people rather than for dwarfs.

More recently, in the 1950s, Ford introduced the Edsel, a design based upon the statistical results of a market survey—the ultimate in the committee design approach. The car had a very brief existence. Both the Airflow and the Edsel are justifiably famous as automotive kludges.

Ralph Nader hung the tag of "kludge" on the Chevrolet Corvair and essentially drove it off the market as a result. However, tests completed by the Department of Transportation in 1972 failed to sustain him.

The Hughes plywood flying boat of World War II, the famous Spruce Goose, is a classical kludge in the aircraft industry. In fact, it may well be the most elaborate and expensive single kludge in recent history.

There are also management and organizational kludges. These are often more interesting than their counterparts in the world of manufacturing. For example, people generally do not behave or perform in the manner management feels will produce maximum organizational results. Thus, the desired organizational results in fact do not equal the desired organizational results on paper, as expressed by the executive statement of corporate goals. In these conditions it is clear that the system needs a managerial kludge. And what better ones are there than encounter groups and sensitivity training. Both of these developed from psychological group therapy, one of the most important practical applications yet discovered through the Finagle Theory of Special Relativity.

Computer kludges are general and very likely the most abrasive in their effects upon people. For example, every single person in the United States is identified by a nine-digit Social Security number. So every person is uniquely identified. But, for computer convenience, all of my credit cards—bank accounts, driver's license, and the like—have *at least* 13 digits and/or letters written in a strange and almost undecipherable format. And they are all different from one another and different from my Social Security number.

The overzealous reaction to kludges in consumer products

has been called *Naderoticism.*[18] On Earth Day I a group of California ecofreaks buried a brand-new automobile. That is one manifestation of Naderoticism. In mid-1972, Mr. Nader visited Australia. With his customary ability to attack the status quo, he made a number of remarks highly critical of Australia and things Australian. This brought forth a rejoinder from Prime Minister William McMahon who called him "a professional and paid pot-stirrer." The newspaper *The Sydney Sun* agreed, saying "the Prime Minister spoke up beautifully, succinctly, and splendidly offensively." That is also Naderoticism.

Conversely, the executive fear of producing a kludge in his manufactured products is often called *Naderphobia.*[18] This disease is approaching near-epidemic proportions in the industrial blunderland of the automotive industry as recalls approach 100 percent. But all companies are vulnerable as computer control is increasingly required to replace people priced out of employment by union militancy and by continual increases in the minimum wage.

For the young executive or engineer, not yet infected by Naderphobia, the creative practice of advanced kludgemanship is an important talent, whether inherited or learned. It can often make the difference between entrapment in the lower reaches of the bureaucracy or early achievement of a vice-presidency.

Anyway, Murphy greatly influenced Finagle. This influence, coupled with his broad experience with kludges, led Finagle to the formulation of two new laws which were based upon Murphy's work, but with slightly different foci.

Finagle's Laws

First Law—*The likelihood of a thing happening is inversely proportional to its desirability.*[2]

Second Law—*Once a job is fouled up, anything done to improve it only makes it worse.*[3]

Finagle's First Law is really the definition of the human experience—what ought desirably to happen never does, and vice versa. For example, the most desirable thing that most of us could imagine would be for taxes to be reduced along with government spending. And we all know how likely that is.

Finagle's Second Law—once a job is fouled up, anything done to improve it only makes it worse—defines the principle of *counterproductivity*. It is an unhappy fact that there are too many poor people in the United States. These people have less money than the rest of us. Clearly, we could make them un-poor by giving them money. But that's too simple and it goes against the national grain—it just isn't right to give money away. Instead, the nation provides the poor, through multitudinous welfare agencies and programs, with services instead of money. And it takes an awful lot of well-paid middle-class bureaucrats to deliver these services. So, instead of helping the poor people become unpoor, welfare programs end up providing many jobs for the middle class.

An even better, more poignant illustration was recounted in *Time*, the Weekly Newsmagazine, on October 16, 1972. In an article discussing the recently authorized twenty percent increase in Social Security benefit payments to the elderly, the case of Mrs. Mary Freed was described. Mrs. Freed is sixty-five years old and suffers from heart disease as well as diabetes. Her monthly Social Security check increased by $27. The increase raised her monthly check to $162.40 per month, just enough to make her ineligible for other forms of welfare. For example, she lost $22 a month in disability insurance, the rent on her public housing apartment went up $7 a month, and she temporarily lost her Medicaid eligibility and had to assume payments to doctors of $14 a month. So, by increasing Social Security benefits, Congress succeeded in reducing her income by about $16 per month.

Finagle was a mere broth of a boy when he first formulated his laws. Contemporary scholars predicted a bright future for this precocious young man. Unfortunately, before reaching maturity he contracted a serious infection of the jocular vein and, poor lad, he never recovered—struck down by a fickle fate just as his talents were reaching their peak.

Frank Wozencraft was obviously not a countryman of either Finagle or of Murphy. Moreover, there is clear evidence that he was unfamiliar with their work. But there is little doubt that his research was closely allied.

Wozencraft's Law

If you make all of your plans on the assumption that a particular thing won't happen—it will.[112]

While this is clearly similar to Finagle's First Law, Wozencraft does describe the phenomenon in more common terms. Everyone, at one time or another, has planned a picnic or a backyard party assuming that it wouldn't rain—but it did. Every executive has made a business plan assuming a certain general trend for sales, or for labor costs, or for inventory—which didn't materialize.

It is clear that Wozencraft, Finagle, and Murphy were all dealing with different manifestations of the same effect. It also demonstrates an occurrence frequent in the natural sciences: that the same scientific discoveries tend to be reported by different people at about the same time, but without either discoverer knowing of the other's work.

In an age of determinism, Calvinism, and Newtonian mechanics, it is hardly surprising that Murphy, Finagle, and Wozencraft concentrated upon the *inevitability* of events proceeding to go wrong. While their laws are confirmed generally by daily happenings, it is clear that all three men shared a failure common to scientists before the emergence of the social sciences; they failed to account for the possibility of direct human intervention. Of cou , this human intervention can be any one, or combination, of several forms:

(1) the exercise of human judgment, which is generally faulty; or

(2) outright error; or

(3) the very human desire to foul things up just for the hell of it.

The omission of the potential for human intervention is quite a gross error that not even a psychologist would make. A man named Rudin, whose identity is unknown to me, was the first to recognize the seriousness of this deficiency. His research centered upon the first form of human intervention: the exercise of individual judgment, which is frequently faulty.

Rudin's Law

Version 1—*In a crisis that forces a choice to be made between alternative courses of action, most people will choose the worst one possible.*

Version 2—*If there is a wrong way to do something, most people will do it every time.*[4]

Both versions of Rudin's Law can be illustrated precisely, thanks to the advantage of hindsight. Certainly the Gulf of Tonkin incident in President Johnson's administration precipitated a major crisis. As a consequence, he and the Congress elected to commit major elements of American military ground forces to action in South Viet Nam. This is certainly in accordance with the first version of Rudin's Law governing the selection of the worst choice possible. It also complies with version 2, that people will invariably choose the wrong way to do something.

It will be apparent later that Rudin's Law was a significant step forward in the development of a comprehensive theory of mistakes, mishaps, and delay. It prompted Thoreau to make his memorable contribution to this newly developing field of study.

Thoreau's Law

If you see a man approaching you with the obvious intent of doing you good, you should run for your life.[5]

For example, I was having trouble with grub worms eating the roots of my grass, ruining the lawn. My friendly neighbor offered to help me out by spraying my yard with the appropriate poison. He killed the grub worms to be sure. He also killed two of my prized oak trees.

The United States Army has a well known adaptation of Rudin's Law. This specialization was, and still is, taught in every Officer Candidate School.

The Army's Law

An order that can be misunderstood will be misunderstood.

Rudin's Law proved to be pivotal in the development of an all-encompassing general theory. However, he considered only the exercise of human judgment in the selection of one of several alternatives.

Edmund C. Berkeley, who was building upon Rudin's research, did account for the second type of human intervention—the common phenomenon of outright error. His results are embodied in two laws and two corollaries.

Berkeley's Laws of Mistakes

First Law—*The moment you have worked out an answer, start checking it—it probably isn't right.*[6]

Corollary 1—*Always let an answer cool off for a little while—it should not be used while hot.*[121]

Corollary 2—*Check the answer you have worked out once more—before you tell it to anybody.*[121]

Second Law—*If there is an opportunity to make a mistake, sooner or later the mistake will be made.*[6]

The average reader may feel that the effects of human intervention have been overstated. But this is simply not so. On May 29, 1972, *The Dallas Morning News* carried a story datelined Detroit with the following headline: "Automaker's Soaring Goofs Blamed on Human Element." The story that followed included this statement:

Almost half as many automobiles have been recalled for inspection and correction of suspected defects as have been sold in the United States since the National Highway Safety Act became law in 1966. The figures roughly are 55.2 million sold and 25 million recalled. . . .

One can only stand in awe of such creative kludgemanship applied on such a grand scale.

Human error affects all aspects of our daily lives. Frankly, I

The Dallas Morning News, Friday, December 1, 1972

Tom Stafford Promoted To Brigadier General

SPACE CENTER, Houston (AP) — Veteran astronaut Thomas P. Stafford has been promoted to the rank of brigadier general in the Air Force. The 3-time space veteran bcomes the youngst officer of flag rank in any of the U.S. services.

The promotion was effecive Friday, thepce agnch nninced STANFOD,½¼ I nseving m pih mto o n ovnrt tn t mmn ogopnvvnt,o voi t mron the astronaut crops.

Stafford is considered to be one of the prime candidates for command of the American crew during the joint Soviet-United States manned space missim on pnoovv vterotomegttndmvethmastronaut to reach flag rank. Astronaut Alan B. Shepard was promoted to rear admiral in the Navy in 1971 and astronatu

JamesA. Mcmi an R gootce gggigggadier general in March, 1972. McDivitt has since retired from the space agency and the Air Force.

Stafford's three space flights were Gemini 6 in 1965, Gemini 9 in 1966 and Apollo 10 in 1969. As commander of Apollo 10, Stafford flew the lunar module to within nine miles of the LUNAR SURFACE IN A DRESS REHEARsal for the first moon landing later that yer.

Stafford is a native of Weatherford, Okla., and a 1952 graduate of the United States Naval Academy. He was selected for the astronaut corps in 1962 after serving as an instructor at the ir Force experimental flight est school at Edwards Air Force Base.

He is married and hastwo children.

---

am constantly amazed by the precision and speed of the people who turn out the daily newspapers. There are occasional misprints and typographical errors, to be sure, for perfection is neither expected nor achievable. But some classic SNAFUs do occur. The one reproduced on the facing page, which must be read in its entirety, is possibly the best recent example.

All of the work reported up to this point has derived from theoreticians—Murphy, Finagle, and the others. Generally, theoreticians are always at odds with experimentalists, usually differing by one or more Finagle Factors. However, experimentalists in both the physical and behavioral sciences long ago discovered that the phenomena of mishap and error described by the laws of Murphy, Finagle, et al., also appear in the laboratory under the most carefully controlled of conditions, just as they do in human affairs. Dr. Lee Harrisberger, presently Dean of Engineering at the University of Texas at Permian Basin, was the first to make an extensive study in the experimental sciences. He compiled the work of several investigators, summarizing and generalizing as follows:

Harrisberger's Laws of the Laboratory

Lowery's First Law—*If it jams—force it. If it breaks, it needed replacing anyway.*

Zumwalt's First Law—*The probability of failure is directly proportional to the number and importance of the people watching the test.*

Second Law—*No matter what result is anticipated, there is always someone willing to fake it.*

Third Law—*Experiments should be reproducive. They should all fail in the same way.*

Fourth Law—*Experience is directly proportional to the amount of equipment ruined.*[110]

Dobbins' Law, which is familiar to every mechanic and technician, is a generalization of Lowery's First Law.

Dobbins' Law
When in doubt, use a bigger hammer.[115]

The laws of Dobbins and Lowery provided the stimulus for Dr. Jack P. Holman's now-famous First Homily.

Holman's First Homily
When in doubt
Make it stout
Out of things
You know about.

Although conceived originally for engineers, Holman's advice has achieved ever-widening acceptance and an ever-increasing generality of interpretation in many different fields.

Zumwalt's First Law received its most striking demonstration in recent years when Lockheed finally gave its first public demonstration of the mammoth and controversial C-5A air transport it is building for the Air Force. With most of the really big brass from Washington on hand in the reviewing stand and with complete coverage by all major television networks, the C-5A landed gracefully as cameras recorded the event for the millions of viewers. Just as the wheels touched the runway, two of them, as I recall it, fell off the airplane and went bouncing down the runway in full view of the audience.

As a consequence of these and other related observations it is now commonly believed that the last form of human intervention—the usual human desire to screw things up just for the hell of it—is nothing more than the ordinary day-to-day practice of basic kludgemanship.

It should be evident by now that these laws, from Murphy through Harrisberger, are somehow related to one another. While this may be intuitively obvious and was taken for granted for many years, it was Professor Francis P. Chisholm who established the relationship definitively and explicitly. He showed that all these laws were simply different manifestations of the same phenomenon, which is now known as *The Chisholm Effect* in his honor.

The Chisholm Effect and the Laws of Human Interaction

First Law—*If anything can go wrong, it will. (This is Murphy's First Law.)*

Corollary 1—*If anything can't go wrong, it will anyway. (This is Murphy's Third Law.)*

Second Law—*When things are going well, something will go wrong.*

Corollary 1—*When things just can't get any worse, they will. (This is Murphy's Second Law.)*

Corollary 2—*Any time things appear to be getting better, you have overlooked something.*

Third Law—*Purposes, as understood by the purposer, will be judged otherwise by others.*

Corollary 1—*If you explain so clearly that nobody can misunderstand, somebody will.*

Corollary 2—*If you do something you are sure will meet with everyone's approval, somebody won't like it.*

Corollary 3—*Procedures devised to implement the purpose won't quite work. (This is kludge implementation.)*[7]

It is necessary now to digress for a moment to engage in a more thorough discussion of Corollary 2 to Chisholm's Third Law—that, if you explain so clearly that nobody can misunderstand, somebody will. This involves the notion of *communication*. The purpose of communication is to achieve understanding. The lack of understanding leads to *confusion*. It may come as a surprise to the nonscientist reader, but *confusion* can be measured quite precisely. In fact,[81] the second law of thermodynamics states that confusion is always increasing in the universe. Of course, the scientific word for confusion is *entropy*. The ideas conveyed by both words are the same, so the more common term, *confusion*, is used here. This similarity of word meanings led Dr. W. L. Everitt, Dean Emeritus of the College of Engineering at the University of Illinois, to restate the second law of thermodynamics to apply to blunderland.

Everitt's Form of the Second Law of Thermodynamics

Confusion (entropy) is always increasing in society. Only if someone or something works extremely hard can this confusion be reduced to order in a limited region.

Nevertheless, this effort will still result in an increase in the total confusion of society at large.[81]

This law is easily demonstrated through the simple process of comparing the state of the country, your city, your job, your family, your recreation, or whatever, as it is today to what it was ten years ago.

It is commonplace to observe the many efforts made to reduce confusion and produce order in organizations. Most such efforts involve attempts, in one form or another, at communication. The theories of information and communication are well understood in the physical sciences, and Everitt translated these results into a format appropriate to blunderland. He particularly noted one law in Claude E. Shannon's pioneering work on communication theory. According to this very fundamental law, if the amount of information supplied to a communication channel exceeds the capacity of the channel to accept or transmit it, then *communication ceases.* (Note that communication is not reduced—it ceases entirely.)

In reflecting on this basic law in electrical engineering, Everitt was struck by how well it explained many of the sources of confusion in the executive blunderland.

Everitt's Corollaries to Shannon's Law

Corollary 1—*Publications are communication channels serving to transmit information from the author to the reader. If the information presented exceeds the individual's capability to absorb it, communication ceases—confusion results.*

Corollary 2—*The modern flood of publications contributes more to confusion than to understanding in the world.*

Corollary 3—*Too large an amount of information presented to a committee can overload it, unless great care is taken, causing the work of the committee to contribute to confusion rather than to order.*[81]

Everitt's work has done much to substantiate Chisholm's Laws in areas where support has clearly been absent in the past. But, even more important, Everitt was the first to translate important theories and concepts from the physical sciences into forms appropriate to the bureaucratic blunderland.

Everitt's general results stimulated an investigation into the role of the educational establishment in this problem area—does it contribute to confusion or to communication? For example, consider the case of a university. Here the academic *courses* represent that which is to be transmitted to the student. The academic *departments* of instruction serve as the communication channels. Obviously, then, when departments offer too many courses confusion is bound to ensue in accordance with Shannon's Law.

The validity of this concept was investigated by Dr. Joel Hildebrand, Professor of Chemistry at the University of California at Berkeley. He found that his Chemistry Department, which was generally regarded as one of the two or three best in the world, listed only seven graduate courses in the University catalogue. In contrast, another school on the same campus, and one generally recognized as a "degree mill," had seventeen *pages* of graduate courses in the catalogue. It was obviously contributing more to confusion than to education. Thus he discovered what is now famous as Hildebrand's Law.

Hildebrand's Law

The quality of a department is inversely proportional to the number of courses it lists in the catalogue.[94]

Clark Kerr, who was then Chancellor of the University of California, was very impressed with Hildebrand's work, but felt that Hildebrand had missed some of the fine structure of a very important and closely related phenomenon. In Kerr's view, Hildebrand had clearly glossed over the entire matter of the number of faculty members in the department, how this factor relates to the total number of course offerings, and the consequent degree of confusion being created. Kerr undertook to correct this oversight through a detailed analysis of university catalogs. His First Law is the result of that work.

Kerr's First Law

The number of courses in the catalogue is equal to twice the number of faculty.

Corollary—*At least one course listed by a faculty member will be his doctoral dissertation.*[94]

Kerr, Hildebrand, Everitt, and Chisholm are rightly regarded as giants in this field of science, standing with the legendary Peter and Parkinson. However, as is true with all scientific laws, they describe only *what* happens without probing or explaining *why* it happened at all.

Of course, by its very nature, science deals only in descriptions of phenomena—scientists are reporters of what happens, not commentators who seek to interpret causes. Thus, Chisholm, et al., rightly stuck to reporting what happens. Not surprisingly, it was a professional commentator, Eric Sevareid, who felt that he had a simple explanation of why things go wrong.

Sevareid's Law

The chief cause of problems is solutions.[8]

The simplicity of Sevareid's Law belies its overwhelming importance and generality. It should be clear to even the most casual observer that the United States is not suffering from too many problems. No, we are suffering from an overwhelming excess of solutions. If the politicians would just stop inventing solutions our problems would largely go away. And if the communications media would just stop telling us about the proposed solutions, national confusion would largely disappear. Indeed, if we take a *really* detached view of contemporary life, or any small facet of it, it appears to be populated by large numbers of people scurrying about with prefabricated solutions in hand, madly searching for problems to which they can be applied. In fact, in more and more instances, problems are defined in terms of available solutions rather than in terms of the parameters of the problem itself.

Vice President Spiro T. Agnew was completely wrong. Our problems are not caused by the "nattering nabobs of negativism" —far from it. The nation's ills are the result of too many provocative purveyors of panaceas—those experts who have all of the answers if only they could find the right questions. The potential hazard is fearful. Canned solutions, like canned food, need precise preparation, and they have a limited shelf life. Unless watched with great care, canned solutions generally go bad and lead to the one disease most feared by executives in blunderland—*botchulism*,[141] *which is a case of consistent, continuing, and unintentional kludgemanship.*

Under the circumstances, it's no wonder that contemporary man tends to general surliness in most interpersonal activities. But on rare occasions the exception occurs and a happy, cheerful soul appears, a person who has the ability to smile through adversity, through the glitches, kludges, SNAFUs, and confusions of life. This is an extraordinarily engaging quality appearing in only a few select people. Its cause was discovered only recently, but the name of the discoverer is shrouded in mystery. However, a leading management consulting firm has shown that there is a probability of 86.73 percent that his name was Jones. And according to Jones:

Jones' Law

The man who can smile when things go wrong has thought of someone he can blame it on.[9]

Jones' Law probably accounts for the majority of such cases. But there is a significant fraction of people who smile because, in their view, the problem of the glitch does not exist. Moreover, they believe that kludgemanship is nothing more than good old American know-how. Jerome Cohen, a professor of law at Harvard University, was deeply interested in this group of people. Being a lawyer, he correctly deduced that, in the end, it really made little difference whether things *actually* go wrong or not. What does matter is whether or not people *think* they went wrong. This insight led to Cohen's Law.

Cohen's Law

Everyone knows that the name of the game is what label you succeed in imposing on the facts.[46]

Cohen's Law has an obvious and particular applicability to politics. It received its most extensive experimental verification during the 1972 Presidential campaign and the primaries that preceded it. Additionally, the periodic official pronouncements on the progress of the war in Viet Nam, throughout its long and unhappy history, provide one of the most illuminating examples of the practice of Cohen's Law. The events and subsequent actions in the notorious Watergate affair provide other outstanding examples.

Although Cohen's Law has been proven only in the special areas just cited, no one doubts that it is widely operative throughout the length and breadth of blunderland. Indeed, when practiced adroitly, the need for Finagle Factors and kludges disappears because the *actual results* are somehow always proven to be the *desired results*.

There is still another way to achieve the *desired results* without recourse to either Cohen's Law or kludge implementation. Rather, in this technique, one simply works within the intrinsic, internal illogic of one or more *established* kludges, with their supporting Finagle Factors, and carries through to the inevitable consequence—a first rate SNAFU.

Recall Granholm's definition of a kludge—an ill-assorted collection of poorly matching parts forming a distressing whole. This is a particularly precise description of taxation systems, all taxation systems in all countries. Such systems are obvious, monumental governmental kludges.

In addition, the cost of all government increases every year as each bureau chief applies his annual Finagle Factor to the forthcoming budget. The ever-increasing government expenditures cause continuing inflation. Inflation is then defined in terms of the cost of living index, a very important Finagle Factor itself. The combination of the kludge (taxing system) with an important Finagle Factor (cost of living index) leads to a classic SNAFU.

Let us now consider the case of Mr. Harry Hyams, as described by Fred Coleman in an Associated Press story from London dated June 28, 1972. It seems that Mr. Hyams spent slightly over $10 million on a thirty-three-story office building complex called Centre Point, in London. It was completed in 1964. The buildings are vacant today and have always been vacant. But let Mr. Coleman tell the story:

When it was built, Centre Point office space could have commanded rentals of $11.20 a square foot for a lease of 15 years. Today the same space would rent out for $18.40 a square foot.

Because of the acute shortage of office space in central London, the *potential* rental income of Centre Point kept skyrocketing as long as the building stayed empty. So did the shares of the property company in which Hyams is the main stock holder. That is how he made his money.

Furthermore, because the building was empty, Hyams paid far lower property taxes on it than he would have paid if it were rented. And the resale value of the building also increased to more than $52 million, a profit over construction costs of about 400 percent.

The British government finally decided to raise his taxes or compell Mr. Hyams to rent the space. But, according to Mr. Coleman, Hyams still has several options.

According to one theory he could tear the empty buildings down and reconstruct [them] on the same sites. By the time they are finished they would command even higher rentals.

And that is how to live with a kludge for fun and profit.

chapter two

Hierarchiology

In years past when everything was smaller and less complex, *bureaucracy* was a term that applied only to government. Indeed, it specifically defined a method for the conduct of business in government through a system of bureaus, or departments, each under the control and direction of a chief. Each bureau chief reported to another higher bureau chief, and so on, in a regular hierarchical form. Prestige, power, and salary were determined by one's relative position in the hierarchy and the number of people over whom the bureau chief had cognizance. It is obvious, then, that the bureau system has built-in motivational pressures to

(1) increase the number of people in each bureau;

(2) increase the number of bureaus;

(3) increase the number of levels in the hierarchy.

Consequently, every element of the bureaucratic form of organization tends to promote organizational expansion.

Since the turn of the century we have witnessed an enormous expansion in the governmental bureaucracy at all levels—city, county, state, and federal. This has been paralleled by a corresponding rise of large corporations, huge trade and labor unions, tremendous universities and school systems, giant hospital centers, and each and every one has adopted the bureau as its basic organizational element. And so, as individuals were swallowed up in these ever-expanding bureaucracies, society itself largely became a battleground of contending bureaucracies, with every citizen a part of many and the victim of many more.

As Flip Wilson, the TV comedian, put it, "We is sometimes the stuckor and sometimes the stuckee, but we is the stuckee an awful lot more than we is the stuckor." Virtually every facet of life today is controlled, or at least significantly affected, by some bureaucrat who is not answerable to those he influences. Because of his power, and because he is not held adequately accountable, the bureaucrat has developed some unique characteristics that are explored in this chapter.

The executive bureaucrat has a parallel, or an analogue as the scientists put it, in the animal kingdom, in the jackass, one of God's nobler creatures. A jackass is a jackass wherever he may be found. One jackass is pretty much like every other jackass except in certain comparatively trivial details such as degree of cussedness, color, and size.

Male chauvinism is difficult to avoid in this connection. The jackass is a male donkey while the female is known as a jenny. While the essential quality of jackassedness is generally well accepted and understood, whoever heard of "jennyness"?

But, back to the analogy of the donkey (male) to the bureaucrat: There is an essential and clearly recognizable quality of jackassedness that sets them apart from other, even closely related animals. No one, for example, is likely to mistake one for a horse.

So it is with bureaucrats—they are pretty much the same wherever and however they are found, whether in federal bureaus or in private corporations, in educational or in military institutions, in the United States or in Russia. Because of these common characteristics, generalizations can be made and laws of bureaucratic behavior can then be deduced.

The Chinese have known about bureaucrats for a very long time. First, they have had 4000 years or so of bureaucratic history—a world record. And second, by sheer population statistics, they have had more bureaucrats than any other nation. In Chinese writing, the ideogram for a bureaucrat shows "a man puffed up with contentment and a full stomach sleeping siesta-style 臣 under a roof 宀 .... They wrote the character first as 官 and finally as 官 ."[116]

The area over which the bureaucrat presides is a blunderland of delay, confusion, error, mismanagement, and resistance to change. Situation Normal, All Fouled Up—SNAFU. This is the motto and the byword of the bureaucrat. The ability to produce SNAFUS by the creative combination of appropriate Finagle Factors and kludges is that single most essential quality, like jackassedness, that sets the career bureaucrat apart from his other human associates. If he is truly expert, he can eventually be promoted to a 長 官 , which is the chief bureaucrat.

It is the purpose of this chapter to reveal why SNAFU is the bureaucratic motto. The essential characteristics of all bureaucracies, and the bureaucrats themselves, will be outlined in a rather complex collection of laws and principles.

A bureaucracy is a highly organized and structured social arrangement. Any social arrangement, precisely because it is an *arrangement*, necessarily possesses an intrinsic, unique power structure within which individuals are ranked. Rank and authority in some systematic power structure are organic to social arrangements; they always appear in all social schemes, even in the most idealistic commune. Anyone who has ever watched barnyard chickens knows this is true, even if they resent the analogy to people. This has been recognized by ethologists and zoologists for many, many years. Robert Ardrey, although a playright by profession, has achieved international fame as an amateur cultural anthropologist. One of his observations on social structure is particularly apt at this point.

Ardrey's Pecking Order Postulate

Every organized society has its system of dominance. Whether it be a school of fish or a flock of birds or a herd of grazing wildebeest, there exists within that society some kind of status order in which individuals are ranked. It is an order founded on fear. Each individual knows all those whom he must fear and all those who must defer to him.... Consciousness of rank appeared at some very early moment in the evolution of living things.[10]

Consciousness of rank, knowing who is the peckee and who is the peckor, is the first stage in the evolution of a bureaucracy. The pecking order gradually solidifies into a rigid system of dominance, and the concept of rank structure emerges as the principal determinant of bureaucratic form. *Hierarchiology* is the scientific study of the rank structure in the bureaucracies.

Bureaucracies come in a wide variety of shapes, sizes, and hierarchical rank structures. The most popular hierarchical form, by a very wide margin, is the traditional *pyramid* described by Antony Jay in *Management and Machiavelli*.

Jay's First Law

The classic hierarchy [consists of] one man at the top with three below him, each of whom has three below him, and so on with fearful symmetry unto the seventh generation, by which stage there is a row of 729 managers.[11]

The pyramidal hierarchy is as ancient as the Roman Empire and has propagated itself through the millennia with little apparent change of form.

Jay based his analysis upon the "Rule of Three" pyramidal hierarchy. This assumes that each person has three people below him in the bureaucracy. The Rule of Three has always been very popular in military bureaucracies. Although any number

could be used at each level in the hierarchy, there are upper
limits on the maximum number of people that one can have
reporting to him. One of the most critical of these constraints
was identified by Dr. Thomas Jones, President of the University
of South Carolina.

Jones' Law of Hierarchical Limits

*As an administrator, you need to give ten pats on the head for
each kick in the butt. This is the reason for keeping the number of
people reporting to you a fairly small number. Otherwise you will
run out of hands, but still have an overcapacity in feet.*[123]

Actually, it appears that the United States is organized, on
a national basis, into a "Rule of Eleven" format. That is, start-
ing with the President at the top, the next level of eleven includes the principal Cabinet officers and a very few key advisors.
The 121 members in the next level include the 100 members of
the Senate, plus various powerful agency heads, such as the
Director of the F.B.I. And so it goes, all the way down to the
eighth level, by which point we have accounted for the entire
U.S. population as well as all the illegal aliens residing here.
All the national leaders, the top dogs in the government, in industry, and in the other bureaucracies—what is known as "the
Establishment"—are all in the first five levels of the national
hierarchy. This is a total of 177,156 people, less than 0.1 percent of the population. The organization of this national hierarchy is illustrated in Figure 1.

In reality, however, there are no pyramidal hierarchies that
exist in quite the purity of form described by Jay. Actually, as
we all know, each subordinate is horizontally linked by important lines of communication and influence with all other subordinates on the same hierarchical level. When this linkage is

Hierarchical Level	Number of People at That Level	
0	1	
1	11	
2	121	
3	1,331	The
4	14,641	Establishment
5	161,051	
....		
6	1,771,561	The Rest
7	19,487,171	of Us
8	214,858,881	
Total U.S. Residents (Population Plus Illegal Aliens)	235,794,769	

Figure 1: The American "Rule of Eleven" Hierarchy

drawn on the organizational chart, it quickly becomes clear that all hierarchical equals must appear, not on a common level, but on a common *circle*. This was discovered by Martin. Thus, the pyramidal hierarchy, which is so commonly thought to describe most bureaucracies, turns out to be the *Martin Spiderweb* in practically all cases.

As the name implies, this is basically a circular structure with authority increasing as one approaches nearer and nearer the center. It consists of concentric circles uniting hierarchical equals and these circles constantly decrease in size as they come closer to the center. There are additional radial lines of authority emanating from the center. This organizational form recognizes that authority is focused in the chief administrative officer (the spider) at the center and that lines of communication and control form a radial network outward to subordinates. As a result, any perturbation or disturbance at any point in the web-like system is quickly communicated laterally to all peer administrators—but, much more important, also directly to the chief executive spider at the center.

This is an extraordinarily useful and effective system of executive control. It is quickly responsive to any excitation or disturbance at any point in the system, much more so than any other organizational form. The Martin Spiderweb is most effective when the central chief executive officer is very strong minded and strong willed—after all, spiders are cannibalistic—at least the females are. (That ought to give you male chauvinists something to think about.) Weak executives cannot bear up under the strain of so many incoming signals and stimuli. As predicted earlier by Everitt's Corollaries to Shannon's Law, too many input signals create confusion. An excess of signals frequently results because the weak executive has a tendency to fail to make timely decisions, or because he fails to delegate decision-making authority. In either case the results are the same—the spiderweb is excited at too many points by too many problems; too many signals appear at the center and organizational confusion, even chaos, ensues. As a result, the weak executive invariably insists upon decoupling the links between hierarchical equals in an effort to reduce the number of incoming signals assaulting him. When this occurs, the traditional pyramidal hierarchy again appears with the apparent classical purity described by Jay.

The classical pyramidal hierarchy has two characteristics summarized by Jay (and based upon his First Law), which are absolutely essential to an understanding of modern hierarchiology.

Jay's Laws of Hierarchy

Second Law—*Every manager knows that whenever a vacancy occurs above him, the odds are two to one against his being appointed to fill it.... And when he first becomes a manager the chances of his getting to the top are 728 to one against.*

Third Law—*The higher you go, the fewer jobs there are; at every level more and more people are forced out.*[11]

Jay's Second Law applies only to a "Rule of Three" hierarchy. The situation would be even worse with a "Rule of Five," or seven, or eleven. For example, in the "Rule of Eleven" national system discussed earlier, the odds against becoming President are 235,794,768 to one. And the chances of getting into the Establishment are only .075 percent, or one chance out of 1331. Come to think of it, that's not bad.

Jay's Third Law appears to be a special case of Bunk Carter's Law. I do not know who Bunk Carter is or was, but his law was published by Paul Crume, columnist for *The Dallas Morning News*.

Bunk Carter's Law

At any given time there are more important people in the world than important jobs to contain them.[113]

Bunk Carter's Law seems to account, in part at least, for the fact that bureaucracies are constantly expanding. This is so because there are so many important people around that it becomes necessary somehow to increase the number of important jobs. This leads to an increase in vice-presidents, department heads, executive officers, and the like.

Most of the *important* people who are forced to occupy the

unimportant jobs must necessarily spend most of their time and effort proving to all with whom they have contact that the adequate performance of their duties is really beneath their dignity.

In the distant past there were not so many important people. And nearly all of them were in important jobs. But now there are *so many* important people, and so few have important jobs. This creates quite a problem because no one ever knows quite how to treat everyone else—how can one tell whether the other fellow is really important or not? Colonel Gus Peters, speaking in Viet Nam in April 1968, presented the best advice currently extant on how to deal with one's associates in the bureaucracy.

Peter's Perfect People Palliative

Each of us is a mixture of good qualities and some, perhaps, not-so-good qualities. In considering our fellowman we should remember his good qualities and realize that his faults only prove that he is, after all, a human being. We should refrain from making harsh judgments of a person just because he happens to be a dirty, rotten, no good son-of-a-bitch.[122]

It is a seeming consequence of Jay's First Law that a pure and unadulterated pyramidal hierarchy would be essentially authoritarian, concentrating great power in the hands of the very few people at the top. In older, simpler, and more stable times this was true; such organizations succeeded spectacularly in comparatively routine activities. After all, the Roman Empire lasted for quite a while.

However, as social and technological stability decreased, and as change came with greater swiftness, difficulties appeared in the pyramidal hierarchy. As the number of hierarchical levels increased, the time required to detect a problem, define it, communicate it upward through channels, make the decision at the top, establish a new policy, communicate it downward through channels, and then carry out the necessary action, simply became excessive. New problems would arise before the action was taken to correct the old problem. Decisions could not be made at the apex of the pyramidal hierarchy rapidly enough to stay in step with events. In other words, in accordance with Everitt's Corollaries to Shannon's Law, the communication channels became overloaded and confusion resulted.

Thus, the old-fashioned illusion of a controlling dictatorial authority at the apex of the pyramid has largely disappeared. It did not disappear altogether, but it was stretched to near-transparency in many cases. It is only necessary to recall the many failures of university administrations to cope with campus upheavals to know that controlling authority in established bureaucracies has atrophied.

Thus, it is found that the rapid growth of the bureaucracy diffuses authority, rather than concentrating it. The symptoms of this effect were described graphically by Alfred P. Sloan, Jr., who was then a member of the Executive Committee of General Motors, in reviewing the status of the corporation in the depths of the great depression in 1931.

Sloan's Organizational Syndrome

The important thing was that no one knew how much [money] was being contributed—plus or minus—by each division to the common good of the corporation. And since, therefore, no one knew or could prove where the efficiencies and inefficiencies lay, there was no objective basis for the allocation of new investment. . . . It was natural for the divisions to compete for investment funds, but it was irrational for the general officers of the company not to know where to place the money to best advantage.[12]

The Sloan Syndrome has been tacitly recognized for many years as an all-too-common characteristic of pyramidal bureaucracies of all types.

In very recent years, the bureaucratization of society has been subjected ' some very searching studies. Dr. Charles A. Reich, of Harvard, articulated the cause of the Sloan Syndrome in his classic study entitled *The Greening of America*. In this, he described the role and function of the "top" executive at the apex of the pyramidal hierarchy.

Reich's Law of Hierarchical Reality

Top executives know only what they are told. In effect, they are "briefed" by others, and the briefing is both limiting and highly selective. The executive is far too busy to find out very much for himself; he must accept the information he gets, and this sets absolute limits to his horizons. Yet the briefing may be three steps removed from the facts, and thus be interpretation built upon interpretation—nearer fiction than fact by the time it reaches the man at the top. The man at the top turns out to be a broker, a decider between limited alternatives, a mediator and arbitrator.[13]

In accordance with Reich and Sloan, the men at the top of *simple* pyramidal hierarchies rarely know what is *really* going on. And every one else in the organization knows that they don't know what is going on.

It is characteristic of bureaucracies that subordinates, who have *no* authority, know precisely what needs to be done, by whom, and in every conceivable circumstance. It is a curious phenomenon of blunderland that as these *same* people are promoted and acquire more and more power they become progressively less sure of what needs to be done. Finally, when they reach the top, they don't have any idea of what needs to be done even though, at last, they have all of the power necessary to do whatever it is that has to be done.

Thus, in a distressingly large number of cases, hierarchical subordinates have only contempt for their bureaucratic superiors. Not surprisingly, realistic authority at the apex of the pyramid vanishes. There is an old Arabian proverb that deals with this problem.

Arabian Proverb

He that knows not and knows not that he knows not is a fool; shun him.
He that knows not and knows that he knows not is a child; teach him.
He that knows and knows not that he knows is asleep; awaken him.
He that knows and knows that he knows is wise; follow him.[131]

The same proverb frequently appears in another, highly Anglicized and bastardized form as follows.

Anglicized Arabian Proverb

The best of all possible situations is to know *that you* know.
The next best situation is to know *that you* don't know.
It is less desirable to not know *that you* know.
But the worst of all possible situations is not to know *that you* don't know.[85]

I am indebted to Professor L. W. Matsch[133] for another statement that follows as a consequence of the foregoing proverb, illustrating the case of the fool. Although the original source is unknown, it is identified here as Matsch's Maxim, accurately reflecting the source here.

Matsch's Maxim

A fool in a high station is like a man on the top of a high mountain—everything appears small to him and he appears small to everybody.[133]

Awareness of the very likely probability that he doesn't know that he doesn't know, that he may be a victim of Reich's Law, usually strikes the individual bureaucrat or executive as a vague sense of unease, a feeling that things are slipping out of his control, a fear that his actual inadequacies will be found out. This can be a real worry, to be sure. But the committed bureaucrat does not take such matters quite this lightly. *Everyone* worries—but executives have major anxieties, and they prove this by having ulcers, heart attacks, and other exotic diseases. These are the merit badges pinned on loyal bureaucrats.

There is an old-fashioned recipe for misery commonly followed by sensitive executives:

Recipe for Misery

> *Take one small worry.*
> *Pat it, cherish it, feed it,*
> *And watch it grow.*
> *It will soon be the*
> *Biggest thing in your life.*[132]

It takes real skill to convert a simple, run-of-the-mill worry into a major, self-destructive anxiety. However, the sincere bureaucrat can, with a little practice and proper attention to the following rules, convert *any* worry into a genuine, full-blown anxiety of substantial proportions. Just follow this process:

How to Convert a Worry into an Anxiety

Step 1—*Figure out the* one *way you could find out if your fears are justified.*

Step 2—*Figure out why the action of finding out is impossible for you to take.*

Step 3—*Figure out why inaction is equally impossible for you.*[107]

The foregoing process always leads to *decision avoidance*, a subject treated in extensive detail in Chapter 3. Indecisiveness makes everyone miserable—the nondecider as well as everyone who is affected by the decision, or its absence. Everyone knows this, even the most cowardly decision-avoider. But, indecisiveness as a basis for *anxiety creation* remains a principal activity of the executive bureaucrat. This is in accordance with a law formulated by Russell Baker, the syndicated newspaper columnist.

Baker's Law

Misery no longer loves company. Nowadays it insists on it.[84]

With a severe worry—or even just a mild anxiety—established, consequent executive response becomes relatively predictable. The most immediate reaction is usually an urgent request for many more reports—usually highly structured in format—more data, more "facts" on which to make decisions which the bureaucrat suspects are on shakier grounds than anyone *really* knows. Fear of making wrong decisions, or decisions that overlook some apparently trivial, but actually important, factor gnaws at his vitals. The production, and continuous updating, of a comprehensive manual of organizational policies and procedures consumes his energies. The design of uniform forms becomes a passion. The mounting flood of reports, studies, computer runs, policy statements and their revisions, and "fact" sheets then requires an assistant, and then another, and his isolation from reality increases yet another step. This causes his fear to increase even more because he knows that he is now even more dependent upon others than he was before. The process repeats itself, one step after the other, in the classical pattern of a positive feedback loop.

This affliction strikes all levels in the hierarchy, not just the very top. It thrives whenever and wherever a potential decider must make decisions on data he did not personally collect—and that includes just about everyone in the organization. The final consequence is well known. It was described precisely by Ward Just writing in *The Atlantic*. He quotes Fitzhugh, who was then Secretary of the Army, in a description of the Pentagon.

The Fitzhugh Phenomenon

Everybody is somewhat responsible for everything and nobody is completely responsible for anything. So there's no way of assuming authority, or accountability. There is nobody you can point your finger to if anything goes wrong, and there is nobody you can pin a medal on if it goes right, because everything is everybody's business. . . . They spend their time coordinating with each other and shuffling paper back and forth, and that's what causes all the red tape and big staffs . . . nobody can do anything without checking with seven other people.[14]

This, of course, is the inevitable consequence of Reich's Law, and it appears in virtually every mature organization. In these cases the individual bureaucrats have been in office so long that their anxieties and fears have infected the entire organizational structure.

Many hierarchiologists, and other students of organization theory, feel that the Fitzhugh Phenomenon, Reich's Law, and the Sloan Syndrome all result from a lack of *communication* between the many and various levels within the hierarchy of the bureaucracy. Clearly, then, according to this line of reasoning, the inauguration of appropriate reporting systems, management information systems, computerized data bases, regularly scheduled and frequent staff meetings, in-house newspapers and bulletins, and the like, will circumvent the Fitzhugh Phenomenon, repeal Reich's Law, and cure the Sloan Syndrome.

While this is certainly well established conventional wisdom, it flies in the face of a large amount of new knowledge accumulated by hierarchiologists. The crux of the matter is whether the *exchange of information* actually constitutes *communication*. There is a difference between the two processes. For example, all of the reporting systems, management information systems, and the other processes listed earlier, and so beloved by management consultants, are simply methods of circulating, collecting, or exchanging information. It is not necessarily true that *communication* is thereby achieved. For example, many years ago the famous Spanish philosopher Ortega y Gasset said:

Ortega on Communication

Between us only a relative and indirect and always dubious communication is possible.[15]

Moreover, whenever there is even a partial lack of trust or candor by either party involved in the proposed communication, and this is apparently almost universally the case in attempts at interhuman communication, a contribution by John Gregory Dunne becomes applicable.

Dunne's Law

The territory behind rhetoric is too often mined with equivocation.[16]

Those of us who have lived and worked in highly structured bureaucracies know that most speeches—and most "factual" reports—tend to be mainly rhetoric. And, sadly, there is a very large amount of equivocation involved in most "official" statements.

Drawn from the earliest beginnings of hierarchiology is the following wisdom:

Communication Theory

I know you believe you understand what you think I said. But I am not sure you realize that what you heard is not what I meant.[17]

These observations received little public attention and had only the slightest effect upon the general theory of organization until collected and analyzed by Martin. These studies led to the formulation of his Law of Communication, which is now regarded as one of the keystones of modern hierarchiology.

Martin's Law of Communication

The inevitable result of improved and enlarged communication between different levels in a hierarchy is a vastly increased area of misunderstanding.[18]

In other words, the more staff meetings that are held, the more coordinators that coordinate, the more in-house newspapers that are published, the more management information systems that are introduced—the more chance there will be for more people to misunderstand the organization's activities. This is not all bad from the bureaucratic viewpoint. More misunderstandings create the need for more people to explain what the organization is doing, and more people means more imposing titles and higher salaries.

Martin's Law of Communication makes it clear that the probability of confusion, and consequent bureaucratic SNAFUS, will increase in direct proportion to the increase in interlevel hierarchical communication. The careful reader will recognize at once that Martin was the first to understand that the multiplicity of attempts at interlevel hierarchical communication—newspapers, bulletins, policy manuals, management information systems, and the like—are nothing more than classic organizational kludges.

Even if Martin's Law was wrong, and even if increased communication did increase understanding, the idea that increased understanding will really help matters by stirring anyone to action completely violates a law formulated by Andrew Hacker in his book *The End of the American Era*.

Hacker's Law

The belief that enhanced understanding will necessarily stir a nation (or an organization) to action is one of mankind's oldest illusions.[19]

Hacker went wrong, in some respects. He used the words "enhanced understanding"—and understanding is something that no one can measure with precision. It is probably true that enhanced understanding, if it actually occurred, would stir people, organizations, and nations to action. But *understanding* infers *real communication* between communicators of identical systems of values and semantics. This almost never occurs. Instead, as noted before, information is transferred, and the

evaluation of this information by the receiver invariably leads
to conclusions different from those intended by the sender.
The consequent action, if there is any at all, is very often
virtually the reverse of that originally intended by the sender.

On balance, then, Martin's Law of Communication proves
that the Fitzhugh Phenomenon is a natural consequence of
Reich's Law. It cannot be circumvented by any of the usual
"communication gap" kludges traditionally suggested.

So far, the discussion in this chapter has centered upon the
consequences of Jay's First Law, the one describing the basic
structure of the pyramidal hierarchy. While it has been shown
that these consequences are important, the greatest contributions to hierarchiology are derived from Jay's Second and Third
Laws. These deal, as you recall, with the very small chances
for promotion when a vacancy occurs in the hierarchy. Jay
was the first to recognize the inevitable consequences of these
two laws in what is identified here as his Hierarchical Syndrome.

Jay's Hierarchical Syndrome

*A man strives for promotion and reward and success up to a cer-
tain point, but, earlier or later, almost all realize that whatever they
do they are not going to get much further. Some will leave; a great
many of the rest reach a switch-off point where they say to themselves, "The difference between going on bursting my guts and taking
it easy is about $1000 a year before taxes. So I'm not going to try."
They then change from aiming at the maximum possible to the minimum excusable.*[20]

The lavish retirement programs of our federal civil service employees encourage the development of Jay's Hierarchical Syndrome.

Jay's Syndrome produces a second-order effect, the need for additional people. This was first noted by Hacker and proved to be the initial step toward the great studies completed by Parkinson and Peter. Hacker studied the need for people in the hierarchy to determine the relationship between these requirements and the proposed work, whatever it might be.

Hacker's Law of Personnel

It is never clear just how many hands—or minds—are needed to carry out a [particular] ... process. Nevertheless, anyone having supervisory responsibility for the completion of the task will invariably protest that his staff is too small for the assignment.[21]

The reason for this is fairly easy to understand. With the protest made, with the record showing that not enough people were available, failure is probable and easy and honorable to accept. The blame is obviously transferred to those who refused to provide the needed manpower. On the other hand, should an improbable success ensue, the bureau chief can modestly accept plaudits for outstanding accomplishments through superior leadership of his undersized and overworked staff.

It is likely that Hacker's work provided the stimulus for the subsequent investigations by Charles R. Vail, who is a vice-president of Southern Methodist University. Actually, Vail's studies marked a significant turning point in hierarchiology, perhaps *the* critical point. Although he himself was unaware of the uniqueness of his approach, Vail undertook to study *work* in the bureaucracy—something few had ever thought to do before; in fact, something no one had ever particularly associated directly with bureaucracies. Vail's research results were embodied in a series of axioms and propositions.

Vail's Axioms

First Axiom—*In any human enterprise, work seeks the lowest hierarchical level.*

Second Axiom—*The percentage of work that remains uncompleted is invariant.*

Corollary 1—*The amount of work to be done increases in proportion to the amount of work already completed.*

Corollary 2—*The amount of material to be filed increases in proportion to the amount already filed.*

Corollary 3—*The amount of material to be purged from the files increases in proportion to the amount already purged.*[22]

Vail's perceptiveness has not been as generally recognized as the importance of his contribution warrants. His two Axioms reveal very clearly that, at every hierarchical level, work is always incomplete, and, necessarily, more people are required to finish it. This fully explains Hacker's Law of Personnel while tracing the consequences of Hacker's Hierarchical Syndrome.

Vail's Second Axiom, that the percentage of uncompleted work is constant, is the critical one. This is apparently based upon the earlier work of Earl Gommersal in the *Harvard Business Review,* which deals with the well-known *Backlog Syndrome.*[119] This describes the common phenomenon that people must have a backlog of work always pressing for completion. Without this there is neither incentive nor enjoyment to daily work. If there is no backlog there is no work to do, and if there is no work to do one is not needed. To assure one's sense of personal importance and value it is essential, therefore, that the demand for one's services shall be unremitting and the backlog of uncompleted work must never disappear. Clearly then, the higher one's UQ (Uncompletion Quotient), the higher is one's backlog and the greater is one's importance. Logically, then, the further behind one gets, the more rapidly one is promoted to higher levels in the hierarchy.

The Second Axiom is the critical one because, properly applied, it explains many key phenomena now grossly misinterpreted by scientists cultivating other fields. For example, because work is never completed at any level in the hierarchy, as Vail observes, the bureaucracy must always expand in an effort to attempt completion. This is evidence of the *Everest Syndrome—because it is there*. But the more the bureaucracy expands, the more work is left undone. Thus, once created, bureaus or departments or divisions, or whatever they may be called, never die, they just keep on expanding. It is necessary, accordingly, for the human population to continue to increase, for otherwise there would be no one to staff the ever-expanding bureaucracies. So we have proved that the population explosion is not a biological problem, but a hierarchiological one. Proponents of zero population growth would do well to ponder the implications of Vail's Second Axiom before they push their program too far.

The Second Axiom similarly proves that the environmentalists and ecologists are also on the wrong track. As we have seen, the population must continue to grow without limit to staff the ever-growing bureaucracies. In addition, everyone must work harder in an effort to complete that part of the work that is always incomplete, to file that material not yet filed, to purge those files not yet purged. In the process more energy is consumed and more of *all* products are used. Thus, air and water pollution and all of the other problems described by environmentalists and ecologists result. It should be obvious that bureaucracy, not misapplied technology, is the cause of the environmental problems we face.

Vail's Proposition, which follows, is derivable from the First

and Second Axioms. While it is not, therefore, a unique addition
to hierarchiology, it is an interesting observation.

Vail's Proposition

*Each individual has a characteristic uncompletion quotient; this
is often called the UQ.*

Lemma 1—*The UQ of each individual is inversely proportional to
his rank in the hierarchy.*

Lemma 2—*The composite UQ of an organization is inversely proportional to its standing in the community.*[22]

Vail's Proposition is accurate in general, but superficially suspect in the particular. According to Lemma 1, the higher one's
rank in the hierarchy, the *lower* the uncompletion coefficient.
This appears to be in direct contradiction to the inferences
derived from the Backlog Syndrome which suggested that individual rank in the hierarchy is directly proportional to the
backlog of uncompleted work. But this contradiction is only
apparent, not real. Vail observed correctly in his First Axiom
that work seeks the lowest hierarchical level. Thus, as the backlog of the top executives builds up, it is systematically passed
downward through the hierarchy. This reduces the apparent
backlog of Mr. Big, as Vail's Proposition predicts, even though
his *real* backlog is the biggest and he had the largest uncompletion coefficient.

These far-reaching implications may have been the catalysts
that triggered the definitive works of Professor C. Northcote
Parkinson. Parkinson was certainly one of the first great
popularizers of hierarchiology. In fact, many credit him with
being the founder of this exciting new field of science. To savor
the full flavor and impact of his discoveries it is necessary

to read all of his many works. These provide very thorough and complete documentation in support of his conclusions. Interested readers should consult the original works for these details; only the results are reproduced here.

Parkinson's Laws

First Law—*Work expands to fill the time available for its completion.*[23]

Corollary 1—*Officials multiply subordinates, not rivals.*[23]

Corollary 2—*Officials make work for each other.*[23]

Second Law—*Expenditure rises to meet income.*[24]

Law of Plants—*Perfection of planned layout is achieved only by institutions on the point of collapse. Perfection is finality and finality is death.*[25]

Parkinson's First Law is clearly a useful generalization of Vail's Second Axiom. That is, the time available to complete work at any hierarchical level is proportional to the number of people available, which is proportional to the amount of work undone. With more people available, more work is undone so that even more people must be brought in. Thus, the work performed expands as the man-hours available for its completion increase.

It is clear that it is almost impossible for a bureaucratic organization to die; it can only expand continuously. This fact is closely related to *The Lockheed Phenomenon;* this first manifested itself in 1971 when the government acted to keep Lockheed from going into bankruptcy. It is also known as *The Wilson Effect—What's Good for Lockheed Is Good for America.* In any event, the Lockheed Phenomenon proved two things:

(1) incompetence on a really grand scale can be rewarding; and

(2) large business bureaucracies never die—they just borrow money from the government.

Parkinson's Second Law, that expenditure rises to meet income, is also a natural consequence of Vail's Second Axiom. As we have seen, the bureaucracy constantly expands to complete the work that the Second Axiom says is always undone. Because ninety percent or more of all organizational expenditures are for salaries, it follows that expenditures must also rise continuously—seldom, if ever, inhibited by income limitations. Thus it is found that inflation is caused by hierarchiology and not by economic factors as is so frequently and mistakenly supposed.

Parkinson's Law of Plants is another natural extension of this same line of reasoning. Clearly, perfection of planned layout can occur only when organizational growth has ceased, because only then can one know precisely what is required, for what and by whom. But it has been proven over and over again that bureaucracies cannot fail to grow as long as they exist. Obviously then, because perfection is achieved only with zero growth, perfection can only mean organizational death as Parkinson states.

Actually, the antecedents of Parkinson's First Law, its corollaries, and, indeed, nearly all bureaucratic behavior, are readily traceable to our ancestors among the higher animals. The general phenomenon of the *territorial imperative*, which is common to all primates, is the key.

In the statement that follows, Robert Ardrey is describing the baboon community. However, his description can be made to apply precisely to any well-developed human bureaucratic organization, as well as to the baboon society, by merely inserting the word *bureau* where Ardrey uses *group*.

Ardrey on the Territorial Imperative

As members of a group[bureau] are isolated from all others by territorial animosity so they are welded together by territorial defense. The stranger must be hated, the fellow protected. For the foreigner there must exist no measure of tolerance or charity or peace; for the countryman one must feel at least rudimentary loyalty and devotion. The individual must protect the group; the group, the individual.[86]

Of course, Ardrey was speaking of geographical territory, but the imperative is equally as strong when applied to bureaucratic areas of cognizance—cognizance is a neat word which, in keeping with bureaucratic sensibilities, avoids using the word *responsibility*.

Members of the bureaucracy protect and defend their departmental territories with a fierceness that would put baboons to shame. The stranger, from any other bureau or department, is suspect and uniformly treated with distrust and outright hatred. Conversely, bureau colleagues, like members of the Irish Republican Army, stick together for the common defense of their areas of purview despite the fact that they very commonly loathe one another personally.

The consequences of the territorial imperative, whether in the geographical behavior of the primates, or in the intellectual behavior of human bureaucrats, are neatly encapsulated into three statements identified here as Ardrey's Laws.

Ardrey's Laws

First Law—*It is a law of nature that territorial animals—whether individual or social—live in eternal hostility with their territorial neighbors.*[87]

Second Law—*Warfare comes about only when the defensive instinct of a determined territorial proprietor is challenged by the predatory compulsions of an equally determined territorial neighbor.*[87]

Third Law—*In species after species natural selection has encouraged social mechanisms which seem ultimately to exist for no other reason than to provide conditions for antagonism and conflict and excitement.*[88]

It is doubtful that anyone, anywhere, or in any field of inquiry, has ever written three more descriptive statements about blunderland.

In accordance with Ardrey's First Law, similar or neighboring bureaus or departments—such as Payroll and Accounting in business, or Physics and Electrical Engineering in a university—live in eternal hostility to one another. Such departments, or bureaus, are constantly at war with one another and each suspects the other of imperialistic expansion at the other's expense—this last in accordance with Ardrey's Second Law.

This conflict between adjoining bureaus is a common practical demonstration of the classical two-person game presented in advanced mathematical treaties on game theory. In mathematics this is known as a zero-sum game. In other words, whatever one person gains, the other player loses—and this is a frequent bureaucratic view of life. This degenerates invariably into an endless game of administrative maneuvering, of bureaucratic "tit for tat." However, the mathematical theory of zero-sum games is characterized by a saddle-point theorem. That is, if you plot a graph such that the left hand side represents the advantage gained by player A, and the right hand side measures the advantage gained by player B, then the curve connecting the two maximum points will droop in the middle—hence the name "saddle point." This is used to define the *minimax principle*, which is a method for determining how you can minimize your losses (your opponent's gains) while maximizing your gains. This clearly produces the optimum strategy. Martin translated this concept for application to blunderland.

Martin's Minimax Maxim

Everyone knows that the name of the game is to let the other guy have all of the little tats and to keep all of the big tits for yourself.[18]

While the two-person, zero-sum game accurately describes phenomena such as World Wars, it is much too simplistic a view of the bureaucracy where the game involves many, many players. The overall complexity is so great that it has not yielded to mathematical analysis.

Ardrey's Third Law deals with social forms evolving so as to create conflict. Without tension and conflict there would not be any need for higher-level bureaucrats to resolve the problems which grow out of these disputes. Thus, because department head A is constantly engaged in irreconcilable disputes with department head B, a superior division head is needed to preside over them to adjudicate their differences. Thus, internal conflict in ever-increasing amounts is necessary to assure the proper expansion of the bureaucracy, with increasing numbers of important jobs for the ever-increasing number of important people noted by Bunk Carter.

There has been a continuing bureaucratization of higher education so that colleges and universities have tended to become hierarchical organizations with little to distinguish them from their governmental or industrial counterparts. Or at least that is the superficial view. Thus it is that cynics, particularly in university administration, have come to recognize the existence of the academic bureaucracy—the *academ-ocracy*. Not surprisingly, however, the faculty does not share this view, seeing the university instead as an *aca-democracy*—an academic democracy. This divergence in viewpoint is the source of much of the conflict that exists between the faculty and the administration on the campus.

The academic hierarchy, while similar in many ways to all others, does have certain rather special peculiarities to be noted in a moment. As a result, academic hierarchiology is often considered to be a distinct area of specialization for thoughtful research workers.

Martin was one of the first to recognize the very special character of the academocracy. The laws he formulated are essentially specializations of Parkinson's Laws to the unique milieu of the academic world.

Martin's Laws of Academia

First Law—*The faculty expands its activity to fit whatever space is available, so that more space is always required.*

Second Law—*Faculty purchases of equipment and supplies always increase to match the funds available, so these funds are never adequate.*

Third Law—*The professional quality of the faculty tends to be inversely proportional to the importance it attaches to space and equipment.*[18]

While the first two laws are obvious specializations of Parkinson's First and Second Laws, Martin's Third Law, dealing with faculty quality, is unique. It is a fact, demonstrated again and again, that when faculty members *really* want to do research, or develop a new student laboratory, they somehow find the time, the means, and the materials. Thus, when they complain that they are not active in research, or cannot mount an interesting student laboratory program, because they lack adequate or proper equipment or space, the *real* reason is that they lack imagination and resourcefulness—they are poor faculty members and their professional quality is low.

Dr. F. E. Terman, Provost Emeritus of Stanford University, is one of the most prominent students of the academic hierarchy. He was particularly intrigued by Parkinson's Second Law—expenditure rises to meet income—and he studied it in the particular context of the university. His law is now firmly fixed and regarded as among the most important discoveries of this century.

Terman's Law

There is no direct relationship between the quality of an educational program and its cost.[105]

Albert Bowker was one of Terman's assistants. He later became the Chancellor of the City University of New York. By building upon Terman's work he made a most important advance in the study of the academocracy.

Bowker's Corollary to Terman's Law

An awful lot of money is being wasted on every college campus.[106]

Bowker's conclusion has far greater generality than might be suspected. His corollary applies to all education—a lot of money is being wasted in all educational institutions. For example, an item in *The Dallas Morning News* of August 2, 1972, was headlined,[124] "80% Jump Seen For School Costs." The article then went on to say: "The almost 80 percent jump is expected although student enrollment is not expected to change significantly. . . ."

One of the interesting aspects of the evolution of hierarchiology is that the work of Finagle, Murphy, and Chisholm, summarized in Chapter 1, proceeded independently of that by Vail, Parkinson, and the others reported in this chapter. Many people suspected that all of these phenomena, while superficially quite different, were, in fact, related. After all, human intervention is a critical factor in why things go wrong, and the bureaucratic hierarchy is the principal instrument for achieving human intervention and consequent kludge implementation. Clearly, the two areas must be related.

The connection was finally made by Dr. Laurence J. Peter[26] in a brilliant flash of intuitive reasoning and perceptive observation now known the world over as *The Peter Principle*. It will be apparent in a moment that the Peter Principle deals with incompetence. Strange though it may seem, Dr. Peter failed to define incompetence competently. He uses the word to mean the inability to perform assigned tasks regularly and accurately. This definition lacks precision because it identifies only one of several forms of incompetence. To rectify this oversight, incompetence is defined here to mean the practice of advanced kludgemanship, as described in Chapter 1, on a sustained basis.

The Peter Principle

In a hierarchy every employee tends to rise to his maximum level of incompetence.[27]

Corollary 1—*Given enough time—and assuming the existence of enough ranks in the hierarchy—each employee rises to, and remains at, his level of incompetence.*[28]

Corollary 2—*In time, every post tends to be occupied by an employee who is incompetent to carry out its duties.*[29]

Corollary 3—*Work is accomplished by those employees who have not yet reached their level of incompetence.*[30]

Corollary 4—*Supercompetence is more objectionable to a hierarchical superior than incompetence.*[31]

The Principle and its corollaries were proved in detail by Peter and Hull and need not be repeated here. One need only reflect briefly on each to recall many examples from immediate personal experience.

With the publication of *The Peter Principle*, many of the causes of mishaps, delay, and confusion in the bureaucracy were revealed. It was a truly significant step forward.

Peter's perception extended beyond the mere formulation and proof of his principle. He gave specific attention to many fine points that a less rigorous theoretician might have overlooked. For example: his advice for evaluating subordinates is excellent.

Peter's Nuance

You should always ask yourself, "Is the person accomplishing any useful work?" If the answer is:

(a) *"Yes"—He has not reached his level of incompetence and therefore exhibits only the Pseudo-Achievement Syndrome.*

(b) *"No"—He has reached his level of incompetence, and therefore exhibits the Final Placement Syndrome.*

(c) *"Don't know"—You have reached your level of incompetence.*[32]

Peter made two additional contributions which have a very high degree of applicability. Both are derivable from the General Principle.

Peter's Paradox

Employees in a hierarchy do not really object to incompetence. They merely gossip about incompetence to mask their envy of employees who have pull.[33]

Peter's Pretty Pass

In an occupational hierarchy, neither your own efforts, nor the pull of your patron, can help you if the next step above you is blocked by someone at his level of incompetence.[34]

A fairly recent phenomenon in blunderland was also covered by Peter. He noted how often executives switched from one bureaucracy to another—say from being an Air Force general to a post as a university president, or from college president to corporation manager, or from college professor to politician or presidential advisor. This led to the formulation of Peter's Law of Compulsive Incompetence.

Peter's Law of Compulsive Incompetence

When there are not enough ranks in the hierarchy for persons to reach their level of incompetence, they have a strong tendency to sidestep into another hierarchy and reach, in that environment, that level of incompetence they could not find in the old.[35]

It is surprising how rapidly the maximum level of incompetence is reached when bureaucrats move laterally from one type of hierarchy to another. The reason for this remained shrouded in mystery until the essential causes were traced to their origins by Ardrey.

In his book *The Territorial Imperative* Ardrey expands on the idea of two distinctly different cultural forms—the *nation* and the *noyau*. Briefly stated, it is Ardrey's view that the nation is held together by antagonism directed toward the *external* enemy; it is a cohesive brotherhood in which patriotism, self-sacrifice, and internal unity are virtues—a system in which the individual is subordinated to the goals of the group. In contrast, the noyau[102] is "a label for a society of inward antagonism . . . those individuals held together by mutual animosity, who could not survive had they no friends to hate." Ardrey goes on to say that the noyau[103] "is a neighborhood of territorial proprietors bound together by a dear-enemy relationship." In this case, hostility is directed toward the *internal* enemy.

Ardrey was writing about the social patterns among the animals when he described the noyau—among, for example, the sportive lemurs, satin bowerbirds, and, most particularly, the Callicebus monkeys. But, in describing the noyau, he unwittingly gave what is unquestionably one of the most precise descriptions ever recorded of many American universities and government agencies. His observations are identified here as Ardrey's Laws of the Noyau. In reading them, think not of the Callicebus monkeys, nor of the sportive lemurs; think of your alma mater or favorite government agency.

Ardrey's Laws of the Noyau

First Law—*A society founded on family territories, innumerable peripheries, and an unholy complexity of inner antagonisms is a society of remarkable staying power. It is flexible. Lacking heart or head, it is difficult to kill. It may lose a portion of its body this century and get it back the next; in the meantime the absence of an arm or leg goes virtually unnoticed. It is healthy.*

Second Law—*Confronted by a crisis, [it] contains no innate mechanisms to command the loyalty of its members.*

Third Law—*Confronted by an aggressive power, [it] must lose or make deals. Confronted by internal crisis, it must choose between disaster and the despot. Either, of course, it will outlive in a century or two.*[104]

In contrast to the noyau character of governmental and educational bureaucracies, American *business* enterprise is a cultural form that closely follows the nation as defined by Ardrey. The difference between nation and noyau is really a subtle one because both contain hierarchies that are superficially similar and exhibit many common characteristics. The essential distinction arises in the identification of the enemy. In business and industry the enemy is the outsider; but in universities and government bureaus the enemy tends to be internal, in the *other* bureaus and departments. This nation–noyau distinction is one of the reasons that businessmen have so much difficulty in transferring their executive skills from the world of business to the groves of academe, or the pastures of government service. They naively expect organizational loyalty from a united staff, or faculty, seeking common organizational goals and opposed by hostile external forces. They never seem to understand that the faculty, or the bureau staff, is not generally loyal to the organization and is not united because the enemy is within, not without. Thus, unity of action and common purpose are almost never possible in a form even remotely comparable to that found in business and industry. This explains why incompetence is so quickly achieved when individuals move from a bureaucracy of one type to one of a different form.

In accordance with Peter's Nuance, noted earlier, it is sometimes possible to detect incompetence in a hierarchical subordinate. When this occurs, one of two—or often both—methods may be applied to relieve the problem. The first, and easily the most preferred, technique requires that more people be brought into the unit to assist the incompetent incumbent. Thus:

Peter's Spiral

Incompetence plus incompetence equals incompetence—attempts to relieve incompetence increase the number of incompetents and still there is no improvement in efficiency.[36]

When the addition of more hands or minds fails, and it nearly always does, then resort is often made to computers in the frantic hope that these powerful extrinsic aids to advanced kludgemanship can overcome the intrinsic human incompetence. Peter investigated this matter extensively and concluded that computers are made in Man's image and are, correspondingly, not to be excluded from his Principle.

Computerized Incompetence

First Law—*The computer may be incompetent itself—that is, it is unable to do regularly and accurately the work for which it was designed.*

Second Law—*Even when competent itself, the computer vastly magnifies the results of incompetence in its owners and operators.*

Third Law—*The computer, like the human employee, is subject to the Principle. If it does good work at first, there is a strong tendency to promote it to more responsible tasks until it reaches its level of incompetence.*[37]

As the First Law states, computers can be organically and functionally incompetent by themselves. For example, in early December 1972, the Office of Social Resources in Honolulu received a letter from American Express. Although it was signed by Maurice Segall, senior vice president and general manager of the credit card division, it was obviously written by an incompetent computer. The letter was addressed to "Mr. Honolulu

City-County." It started out, "Dear Mr. County," and included a credit card application.

The Second and Third Laws are simply elaborate statements of an old principle of computer science known as GIGO—garbage in, garbage out. Computer outputs are no better than the inputs. A recent illustration was provided by pronouncements by the elite Club of Rome forecasting the total breakdown of society in rather explicit terms—and derived from a computer analysis. This apparently prompted Professor K. William Kapp of Basel University to say:[129]

"Had there been a computer in 1872, it would probably have predicted that by now there would be so many horsedrawn vehicles it would be impossible to clean up all the manure."

In the end, with or without computers, the whole business makes little difference to the career bureaucrat. Safe in his tenured, and/or sinecured, slot in the hierarchy, he daily repeats his motto.

Peter's Placebo

An ounce of image is worth a pound of performance.[38]

Peter's work has been quite substantially extended by Arthur J. Riggs writing in the *Michigan Business Review*. Without repeating all of the details offered by Riggs, it is enough to say that he argues that the Peter Principle presumes a rectilinear, or quantized sort of kinked transition from competence to incompetence. This is a binary theory which assumes only two stable states—competence and incompetence—and does not conceive of a gradual transition from one state to another.

In contrast, *The Riggs Hypothesis*[39] assumes that incompetence increases in a more or less curvilinear form. In other words, as people are gradually promoted upwards through the hierarchy, they progressively and continuously become more incompetent. This is a major departure from Peter's theory which postulates only two states. Moreover, the Riggs theory proposes that most people are characterized by two or more such curves of incompetence, each one rising to a higher level of maximum incompetence than the one immediately preceding it. This is illustrated in the accompanying diagram which was taken from the original paper by Riggs.

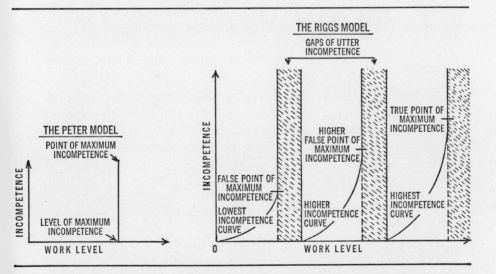

Figure 2: Comparison of the Riggs Hypothesis and the Peter Principle

Riggs correctly assumes that progress upwards through the hierarchy is not a continuous process as described by Peter.

Rather, it is discontinuous and in several stages. For example, a new employee might start out in engineering and, in due course, be promoted to higher and higher levels in the engineering divisional hierarchy. His level of incompetence increases steadily until the first *false* point of maximum incompetence is achieved. Then, he probably moves laterally into another division of the company, possibly to the Personnel Department. Once again he moves upward through *that* hierarchy and along a curve of continuously increasing incompetence. This process can repeat itself again and again with our example employee finally reaching his true point of maximum incompetence as Vice-President of International Sales.

It could well be argued that the Riggs Hypothesis is seemingly only a special case of Peter's Law of Compulsive Incompetence. It is certainly true that there is a close relationship; but the Riggs model differs because of the curvilinear character of the transition to incompetence, and the fact that Riggs assumes continuous employment in the same organization, in contrast to Peter. It is clear, by inference, that Riggs views modern organizations as an involved set of interlocking hierarchies, while Peter clings to the simplistic view of a single monolithic bureaucratic pyramid.

Peter and Parkinson have had a profound influence on hierarchiology—so much so that a significant contribution by Wilkerson, of *The Comanche Chief* newspaper, has languished in almost total obscurity. Wilkerson's approach is quite different.

Wilkerson's Law

The anatomy of any community (or organization) includes four kinds of bones:

Wish-bones—Those who will go along with an idea, but want someone else to do the work.

Jaw-bones—Who talk a lot, but do little else.

Knuckle-bones—Who knock everything everyone else does.

Back-bones—Who get behind the wheel and do the work.[40]

The first three bones are the incompetent, of course, while the fourth kind do all the work and are the few competents.

Over the years the incompetents have developed an extensive list of excuses for failure. The most comprehensive collection was compiled by the Swift Printing Company of New York and provided to me by Edmund C. Berkeley, Editor of *Computers and Automation.*

Swift's Handy List of Excuses for Failure

I didn't know you were in a hurry for it.
That's not in my department.
No one told me to go ahead.
How did I know this was different?
That's his job, not mine.
Wait till the boss comes back and ask him.
I forgot.
I didn't think it was very important.
I'm so busy I just didn't get around to it.
I thought I told you that.
I wasn't hired to do that.
I thought it was good enough.
They will never notice that.[125]

Both the competents and the incompetents can find solace from Dr. William R. Bennett, pastor of the Trinity Avenue Presbyterian Church of Durham, N.C. His first Beatitude is for the incompetents and his second is for the competents.

Bennett's Beatitudes

First—*Blessed is he who has reached the point of no return and knows it, for he shall enjoy living.*

Second—*Blessed is he who expects no gratitude, for he shall not be disappointed.*[41]

Expansion is the bureaucratic imperative. It is therefore inevitable that, as time passes, every position in an organization comes to be occupied by someone at his maximum level of incompetence. This suggests that there is a characteristic life cycle for hierarchies. This was the conclusion of Richard H. Brien.

Brien's First Law

At some time in the life cycle of virtually every organization, its ability to succeed in spite of itself runs out.[42]

On the face of it, Brien's Law would appear to contradict the conclusions of Vail, Parkinson, and others who identified constant growth as an inherent organizational characteristic. But it is obvious that nothing, not even a bureaucracy, can expand forever. Sooner or later some limitations must set in, either because of the increasingly heavy burden of incompetents, or because the Uncompletion Quotient finally reaches "total." Thus, the real truth, or error, of Brien's Law is still unknown. In any event, it appears that for the first time in recorded history civilization has reached a point where the bureaucracies are expanding faster than Man can breed new bureaucrats. Clearly, something has to give eventually, and Brien may yet prove to have the final word.

chapter three

Status Quo Vadis

As noted in the preceding chapter, bureaucracies are indigenous to every nation, every form of government, and every economic system. In a very general way the various bureaucracies can be classified into four major groups: educational, governmental, business, and industry. The last two have their alter egos in the bureaucracies of labor. These four categories overlap one another somewhat and there are myriad subdivisions within each of the general groupings.

In a very early phenomenological study of this broad spectrum of hierarchies, Martin stumbled on to an effect of far-reaching importance and which now bears his name.

The Martin Effect

First Effect—*Executives in the hierarchies of government and education call themselves administrators.*

Second Effect—*Executives in the hierarchies of business and industry call themselves managers.*

Martin's Singular Point—*Executives in the hierarchies of labor are called leaders.*[18]

This administrator-manager-leader identification is a nontrivial distinction, one well worth studious reflection.

The Martin Effect is observed almost universally the world over. This is surprising, superficially at least, because it shows that bureaucratic imperatives are stronger than national or political imperatives. It is even more surprising because the most careful study of the various broad classes of hierarchies fails to reveal any observable differences in the character of the work performed by executives—that is, executives in government serve the same functions and do the same work as executives in business. So, even though they are indistinguishable from one another in what they do, they insist upon differentiating themselves by title. Professor C. Northcote Parkinson, in his later work, did much to clarify this apparent enigma.

For example, Parkinson discovered that *all* hierarchies are populated by two basically different types of bureaucrats—the *Abominable No Man,* who always says no, and the *Willingman,* who tries to solve the problem. It is shown later in Parkinson's book that the administrator tends to be the Abominable No Man, while the manager tends to be the Willingman. Parkinson further discovered that these two types of people tend to alternate through the levels of the hierarchy—every Willingman reports to an Abominable No Man, and vice versa. The trick in getting something done through any hierarchy, Parkinson observes, is to persevere up through the hierarchical levels until you find a Willingman that you can persuade, by hook or by crook, to make the decision himself, then and there, not to pass it upward for review because the next man is surely an Abominable No Man.

Antony Jay's studies, as reported in his book *Management and Machiavelli,* led him to conclusions seemingly different from Parkinson's. But, when examined in careful detail, it becomes evident that they actually agree quite explicitly.

Jay observed that there was a remarkable similarity between the structure and mode of operation of all modern hierarchies and the characteristics of medieval society. In medieval times the royal hierarchy involved a king at the top, courtiers who advised the king directly, and barons who pledged allegiance to the king and who controlled important territories. The barons were important in their own rights because they had large land holdings and commanded the services of numerous peasants capable of bearing arms and being taxed; these are two very consequential facts of life. The courtiers, in contrast, were important *only* because they had direct access to the ear of the king; they generated neither taxes nor armed men. However, whatever advice they gave the king tended to carry much more weight than baronial advice because only the courtier was presumably in a position to fully appreciate the Big Picture—and we all know how important that is.

It will be recognized immediately that this structural form appears at all levels in all hierarchies, where the king is always taken to be the next man higher in the hierarchy. Each executive king has advisors, or courtiers, as well as executive barons who report directly to him. Of course, most of the internal tensions of an organization result from the eternal struggle for power between the courtiers, who have the king's ear, and the barons, who are running the operating divisions of the enterprise. Courtiers are specialists whose performance is judged by the quality of the *advice* they give. Barons are judged by the quality of the *results* they produce.

These alternating layers of courtiers and barons are reproduced exactly in the conventional military hierarchy as the functions of staff and command are interleaved. The resemblance to the alternating layers of the Parkinsonian Abominable No Men and Willingmen is abundantly clear.

It was Dean Martin, the original one from Southern Methodist University, who finally integrated the work of Jay and Parkinson into the three basic Laws of Hierarchical Function.

Martin's Laws of Hierarchical Function

First Law—*All hierarchies contain administrators and managers, and they tend to appear at alternating levels in the hierarchy.*

Second Law—*Administration maintains the status quo.*

Third Law—*Management directs and controls change.*[18]

Thus, Martin showed that the *administrator* is the courtier, the Abominable No Man, and the decision-avoider. In contrast, he shows that the *manager* is the leader, the Willingman, the backbone who makes the decisions. And, in accordance with his first law, both types appear in all hierarchies, generally at alternating levels. With these distinctions established it is a curious fact that executives in government and education persist in calling themselves administrators, while business executives insist —to a man, woman, or person—that they are managers.

It is instructive to look at administrators separately, and in some detail, to gain a clearer perception of these matters. The administrator is always revealed by two characteristics: first, by his insistence upon the preservation of the status quo, as stated in Martin's Second Law; and second, by his insistence upon ever-increasing centralization of all functions below his level in the hierarchy. These characteristics will be reviewed separately in this chapter.

Martin's Second Law, concerning administrative preservation of the status quo, was confirmed by Professor Charles A. Reich in three important laws.

Reich's Laws of Administration

First Law—*Administration means a rejection of the idea of conflict as a desirable element of society. Administration wants extremes adjusted; it wants differences settled; it wants to find which way is best and use that way exclusively.*

Corollary 1—*Whatever refuses to be adjusted is considered to be a "deviance," a departure from the norm that must be treated and cured.*

Corollary 2—*It is a therapeutic model . . . in which variety is compromised and smoothed over in an effort to make everything conform to the "public interest."*

Second Law—*Administration is neutral in favor of the present policy.*

Third Law—*Things go most smoothly when the status quo is maintained, when change is slow, cautious, and evolutionary.*[43]

Reich's Second and Third Laws are essentially restatements and expansions of Martin's Second Law.

However, Reich's First Law describes a characteristic that always distinguishes the administrator from the manager: the desire to find the best way and *to use that way exclusively.* Organizations with voluminous policy manuals, covering every conceivable contingency or action, are clearly in the grip of administrators—not managers. The fact that the mindless "cookie cutter" application of such policies stifles initiative and innovation, that it surely presages organizational decay, is not understood by the administrator.

Sam Rayburn, the former Speaker of the House of Representatives, was a politician of considerable skill. Thus, the experienced administrator, anticipating a long career, is well advised to ponder Rayburn's Rule.

Rayburn's Rule

If you want to get along, go along.[44]

James Boren, President of NATAPROBU (National Association of Professional Bureaucrats) provides the *administrator-*

executive with essential rules of behavior to secure executive success, while maintaining close adherence to Reich's Laws of Administration.

Boren's Laws

First Law—*When in charge, ponder.*

Second Law—*When in trouble, delegate.*

Third Law—*When in doubt, mumble.*[45]

Harry S Truman, the former President, contributed a typically pithy and appropriate comment very closely related to Boren's Laws. Although he had reference to the platform of the Republican party, his law applies very well to the behavior of administrators in general.

Truman's Law

If you can't convince them, confuse them.[101]

Boren's and Truman's Laws are specializations of a larger and more important phenomenon, which is characteristic of the administrative blunderland. This was identified by William V. Shannon in writing about the McGovern candidacy in 1972.

Shannon's Law of Administration

What is actually *happening is often less important than what* appears *to be happening.*[128]

Of course, the behavior described by Rayburn, Boren, and Truman results from bureaucratic efforts at self-protection, attempts to avoid the possibility of making a mistake by passing the buck to someone else. Buck-passing is an old and honored custom, practiced with consummate skill by most government executives. However, one should not overlook some of the really superb examples being demonstrated with increasing frequency on the campuses of many universities and in many business organizations.

In earlier days, and before the technique was fully refined, it was believed that the buck could be passed only up or down —usually, and obviously, passing the buck for *blame* down, and the buck for *action* up. However, serious students of hierarchiology recognized that buck-passing was not purely an up or down phenomenon, that it must unquestionably have three-dimensional possibilities. Thus, it was revealed that really creative buck passers frequently used the *lateral pass* to hierarchical equals with great effect.

It soon became apparent to serious observers that buck-passing, while fun and frequently rewarding, was not actually an end in itself. Rather, it proved to be simply a part of the larger and more complex process known as decision avoidance. In fact, it is now well recognized that "the morbid fear of making decisions" is nearly universal. Psychologists have given this hitherto unrecognized neurosis the name *decidophobia*.[91]

Examples of decidophobia appear with distressing regularity in the columns of the daily newspapers and newsmagazines. For example, in August 1972, the disintegration of the Times Square area in New York City was having a very adverse effect upon the theater business. The concentration and aggressiveness of prostitutes had reached staggering proportions. *Time* reported as follows:

Actress Joan Hackett was appalled by the evolution of New York's theatre district. "Times Square is as evil as it can be," she said. "I was propositioned by a girl who looked about 17.... Working on Broadway is prestige—and it's no longer prestigious to be part of one large massage parlor." Sixty other theatre people...joined Joan in petitioning Mayor John V. Lindsay to establish an official red light district remote from Broadway. After two months, the Mayor solemnly wrote back that the idea might "deserve serious study" but was not "a feasible or workable suggestion at the present time."[126]

Note the two-month delay, the reply that the idea *might* "deserve serious study"—but no suggestion that it would get it—that it was not "a feasible or workable suggestion *at the present time*," which suggests that it might be later. Well, that's decidophobia, and those are some of the typical signals of its presence.

As nearly as can be determined, Lord Falkland was the first to identify decision avoidance as a recognizable phenomenon.

Lord Falkland's Rule

When it is not necessary to make a decision, it is necessary not to make a decision.[47]

With the help of Lord Falkland, Mayor Lindsay, and contemporary psychologists, the phenomenon of decidophobia was delineated at last; a great deal of progress resulted soon thereafter.

Parkinson's identification of the Abominable No Man was noted at the beginning of the chapter. It is appropriate now, in connection with decidophobia, to quote Parkinson at length on this subject because his work is the definitive reference on the matter.

Parkinson on the Abominable No Man

He says "No" because he has found that this is the easiest way and because he never says anything else. Should he say "yes" he might be asked to explain the basis for his enthusiasm. Should he approve, he might be involved in work resulting from the proposal's acceptance. Should the scheme prove a failure he might be held responsible for advocating it in the first place. But saying "No" is relatively safe. It requires no explanations because no action follows. Nor can the scheme fail because it will never be tried ... even later acceptance of the plan need not worry the No Man unduly. He cannot be held responsible for any failure and will not be asked to aid in insuring success. Few will remember his opposition and those who do can be told that the plan in its original form *was impractical and that its effective application after revision owed much to the process of healthy criticism to which it was subjected in the early stages of its development. The No Man has little to lose.*[48]

Parkinson makes it clear that techniques for avoiding a decision have been developed to a high art. Decision-avoiders, those infected with decidophobia, have become more the rule than the exception.

Although all patriotic Americans know that this nation will never take a back seat to anyone, in any thing, at any time, it does appear that decision avoidance has attained new levels of artistry in India, if we are to believe a recent publication by Dr. Sharu S. Rangnekar. Granting Rangnekar's contention of Indian superiority in this area, even a casual examination of his Rules for Decision Avoidance reveal that they have also been practiced in the United States for many years and with consummate skill.

Rangnekar's Rules for Decision Avoidance

Rule 1—*If you can avoid a decision, do so.*

Rule 2—*If you can avoid a decision, don't delay it.*

Rule 3—*If you can get somebody else to avoid a decision, don't avoid it yourself.*

Rule 4—*If you cannot get one person to avoid the decision, appoint a committee.*

Rule 1 is actually an inelegant corruption of Lord Falkland's Rule, but it is more understandable. Rule 1 is the foundation for all truly creative cases of decidophobia.

Rangnekar's Rule 2 is the most difficult of all to follow with a clear administrative conscience. In most cases, delay is essential to the process of avoiding the decision. Thus, the injunction "don't delay it" is almost contradictory. However, Rangnekar means that one should unhesitatingly, without a second thought, promptly and immediately avoid making a decision. This naturally produces delay and is, therefore, one of the most effective methods for eventual and total decision avoidance.

Generally speaking, Rule 2 is implemented through immediate application of Rule 3—that is, get somebody else to avoid the decision, further increasing the delay. To those with mean minds, this may seem to be ordinary buck-passing. But the dedicated administrator knows that Rule 3 is what makes jobs for more and more "important people," like him, and as defined by Bunk Carter earlier.

Rangnekar's Rules are very generally followed in all bureaucracies. Generally in serial order. That is, Rule 1 is tried, followed by Rule 2 and then 3. Finally, Rule 4 is invoked and a committee is appointed. The role of the committee in the theory and practice of decision avoidance is well established. It is one of the most formidable weapons in the extensive arsenal that the administrator can deploy against change. And it is such an easy weapon to use, while graciously accepting plaudits for a democratic approach to organizational problems. The committee is the absolute *sine qua non* of any constituency form of shared governance, which is the modern approach of the emancipated administrator and a sure route to operational chaos.

Comitology, a word coined by Parkinson, denotes the scientific study of committees. Comitologists define the committee variously.

Committee Defined

(1) A collection of the unfit chosen from the unwilling by the incompetent to do the unnecessary.

(2) A group of people who, individually, can do nothing, but collectively can meet and decide that nothing can be done.

(3) A group which succeeds in getting something done when, and only when, it consists of three members, one of whom happens to be sick and another absent.[50]

It has been known for some time—even Parkinson discussed it at length—that committee size is absolutely critical in effective decision avoidance. Rangnekar quantified the matter into a very compact, useful and easily understood law.

Rangnekar's Law of Committee Size

The possibility of avoiding decisions increases in proportion to the square of the number of members on the committee.[51]

Thus, an eight-man committee is four times as effective in avoiding decisions as is a four-person committee, and a sixteen-member committee is sixty-four times as effective. This makes it very easy to determine in advance the proper size of a committee once it is known how important it is to avoid a decision.

Parkinson made a serious effort to determine both the maximum and minimum memberships possible for effective committee operation. Unlike Rangnekar, Parkinson apparently assumed that committees could, on occasion, be effective decision-makers, as long as they did not become unduly large.

Parkinson's Laws of Committee Size

First Law—*A membership of three is too small because a quorum is impossible to collect.*

Second Law—*The [committee] would seem to consist ideally of five. With that number . . . two members can be absent or sick at any one time. Five members are easy to collect and, when collected, can act with competence, secrecy, and speed.*

Third Law—*The point of total ineffectiveness in a committee is reached when the total membership exceeds twenty.*[52]

In accordance with Rangnekar, a committee with twenty members is sixteen times as likely to avoid a decision as one with five, which size Parkinson says is ideal. But it should also be noted that a committee of five is nearly three times as likely to avoid a decision as a committee of three, which Parkinson says is too small.

In his studies of committees, Parkinson also formulated his now-famous Law of Triviality.

Parkinson's Law of Triviality

The time spent on any item of the agenda will be in inverse proportion to the sum of money involved.[53]

Actually, this is an outgrowth of an earlier discovery by Gresham.

Gresham's Law

Trivial matters are handled promptly.
Corollary—*important matters are never solved.*[54]

In recent years the more serious comitologists have come to recognize that there are a number of very close correspondences between the laws of physical science and certain phenomena found in committee operations in blunderland. One such is a well known law in chemistry which deals with the theory of chemical reactions.

The Berthelot Principle

Of all possible reactions, that one will occur which will liberate the greatest amount of heat.[100]

Although the analogous principle in committee deliberations literally screams for recognition, it was identified only very recently and accidentally by Martin, proving that serendipity does exist.

The Martin-Berthelot Principle

Of all possible committee reactions to any given agenda item, that one will occur which will liberate the greatest amount of hot air.[18]

Almost everyone who serves on committees—and who hasn't —knows that committees, like their parental bureaucracies, achieve intrinsic lives of their own. Indeed, one of the more important laws of comitology bearing on this point was formulated as recently as 1971 by Dr. E. R. Hendrickson, President of Environmental Engineering, Inc.

Hendrickson's Law

If you have enough meetings over a long enough period of time, the meetings become more important than the problem the meetings were intended to solve.[55]

Among administrators it is considered very bad form indeed to suggest that the committee is merely a practical device for decision avoidance. Instead, the committee is touted rather glowingly as a pragmatic expression of the *Two-Heads-Are-Better-Than-One Principle*. Obviously then, by the same reasoning, three, four, five, or even more heads are even better. This matter was investigated in detail by William H. Whyte, in his book *The Organization Man*, because there was always the faint possibility that there might be some shred of truth to this common assertion. Whyte failed to find any such evidence; rather, his observations confirmed those summarized so far.

Whyte's Laws of Committee Operation

First Law—*People very rarely think in groups; they talk together, they exchange information, they adjudicate, they make compromises. But they do not think; they do not create.*

Second Law—*A meeting cannot be productive unless certain premises are so shared that they don't need to be discussed and the argument can be confined to areas of disagreement. But while this kind of consensus makes a group more effective in its legitimate functions, it does not make the group a creative vehicle.*

Third Law—*A really new idea affronts current agreement—it wouldn't be a new idea if it didn't—and the group, impelled as it is to agree, is instinctively hostile to that which is divisive.*[56]

The science of comitology recognizes this urge to agree, this need for consensus and the resulting noncreativity of committees. Thus, theoretical comitologists recognize that a regular code of manners has grown out of the need for consensus. This was first noted by Professor Jacques Barzun, who is particularly eminent as a student of the academic bureaucracies.

Barzun's Bywords for Committee Pussyfooting

In the common round of committee meetings, it is necessary to differ, but also impossible. Manners therefore decree that one shall say:
"I may be wrong, but . . ."
"You'll correct me if I'm wrong . . ."
"I'm only thinking aloud . . ."
"It looks that way from where I sit."
"It's only a crazy notion that crossed my mind."[57]

And, of course, there is the ever-popular, "Well, it's only off the top of my head."

Martin's Law of Committees is only a logical and natural outgrowth of these various observations, that committees are not creative vehicles and that committee members invariably pussyfoot.

Martin's Law of Committees

All committee reports conclude that "it is not prudent to change the policy [or procedure, or organization, or whatever] at this time." Martin's Exclusion—*Committee reports dealing with wages, salaries, fringe benefits, facilities, computers, employee parking, libraries, coffee breaks, secretarial support, etc., always call for dramatic expenditure increases.*[18]

On rare occasions the administrative use of the committee gambit at decision avoidance may fail. It may fail because the initiator of the request for a decision may recognize the attempt at decision avoidance and threaten to reveal the Abominable No Man for what he is. Or, the committee may, for some wholly inexplicable reason, actually make a decision. Or the Willingman, who is the supervisor of the would-be decision-avoider, may rule out the use of a committee. Fortunately, Rangnekar does not leave the dedicated administrator unprotected. He provides six techniques which, if practiced with verve, imagination, and appropriate skill, can still allow the decision to be avoided.

Rangnekar's Techniques for Decision Avoidance

(1) Tantrum Method—*When the initiator offers a proposal, throw a tantrum.*

(2) Hush-Hush Method—*Warn the initiator that he is rushing in where angels fear to tread.*

(3) More-Details-Please Method—*Keep asking for more and more details; the initiator will sooner or later abandon his proposal.*

(4) Doubletalk Method—*Use management jargon to confuse the initiator.*

(5) No-Problem-Exists Method—*Deny the very existence of the problem.*

(6) That's-Your-Problem Method—*Throw it back at the initiator.*[59]

There is a well known refinement of the More-Details-Please Method that is usually effective in producing very long delays and an eventual report that cannot be implemented. Thus, it is a very effective technique in decision avoidance. This is the time-honored practice of calling in outside consultants, especially management consultants, who are obviously not managers at all, but consulting administrators. As such, they are consummate masters of producing reports which make decision avoidance almost necessary for organizational survival. Consultants have been defined by some anonymous manager as follows:

Consultant Defined

A man who knows less about your business than you do and gets more for telling you how to run it than you could possibly make out of it even if you ran it right instead of the way he told you.[109]

The final, and most devastating, method of decision avoidance is also the simplest—plain, ordinary, simple delay. Often the committee is the tool through which delay is achieved, though individual administrators are generally very effective on their own. But, in any case, and by what ever method, delay is the ultimate weapon of the Abominable No Man. This was recognized by Professor Parkinson in a recent book.

Parkinson's Law of Delay

Delay is the deadliest form of denial.[60]

Most of us recognize the accuracy of Parkinson's Law from purely personal experience, both as the delayee and the delayor. Readers interested in complete documentation of this law are referred to the extensive presentation by Parkinson in the reference cited.

The imaginative practice of delaying tactics requires a broad spectrum of talents, some of which were overlooked by Parkinson. For example, paperwork and correspondence are the life blood of the bureaucracy and present many opportunities for creative delay.

Never Answer the Letter Laws

First Law—*Never answer a letter until you get a second one on the same subject from the same person.*

Second Law—*Never answer a letter; sooner or later you'll see the writer in person.*[114]

As noted earlier in this chapter, the administrator is revealed by two special characteristics of which insistence upon the preservation of the status quo is one. Thus far, the discussion has centered only upon this factor.

The second major characteristic of administrators is their desire for ever-increasing centralization of all functions in the hierarchical levels below them. Centralized control is always the goal of the palace courtiers (staff, administrators, etc.) in the headquarters of the king. In contrast, decentralization is always the goal of the barons (managers, division heads, etc.). Chaos and eventual organizational destruction are the inevitable consequences if either side wins completely.

Excessive centralization is dangerous because the central administrators are inexperienced in making decisions for which they are singly responsible, but which affect all facets of operations. The administrator's role has been as one of a group giving advice to the king in a comparatively specialized area while studiously avoiding individual decision-making. The administrator-courtier knows that he is inexperienced in decision-making, he isn't stupid. But he lives in constant fear that the baronial managers may produce results, often highly desirable to the king, that turn out to be the opposite from those he had anticipated when he advised the king. This would reflect adversely upon him. To prevent such gross managerial errors and misjudgments, which just might establish the inadequacy of his advice, the administrator invariably insists that all decisions must be made centrally, which, in his view, is the only place where the Big Picture is visible and completely understood. He is naturally suspicious of everything that the baronial managers do, and this leads to the Corporate Headquarters Syndrome, which is also known as the Courtiers' Complaint.

Courtiers' Complaint

What are those bastards up to now?[18]

Dr. Michael B. Shimkin first noted this characteristic in research administrators. At the time Dr. Shimkin was Chief of the Biometry Branch of the National Cancer Institute. He formulated seven principles of research administration which account for this characteristic and several other related factors. Two of these principles are actually applicable to all administrators in any field by simply replacing Shimkin's words "research scientist" with the term "manager." That liberty has been taken here with two of Shimkin's Principles and the following statements result.

Shimkin's Principles of Administration

The Whole Picture Principle—*It is axiomatic that division managers are so wrapped up in their own narrow endeavors ... that they cannot possibly see the Whole Picture of anything, including their own divisions. It naturally follows that big programs ... should be guided not by managers but by trained administrators who can grasp the Whole Picture.*[61]

The Combined Thinking Principle—*It is axiomatic that two heads are better than one, and a dozen is a nice even number. Given administrative practices require that Directors have councils, consultants, and committees ... if anything goes wrong, the responsibility*

*can be graciously divided and erroneous decisions supported by the
full minutes of the committee.*

Shimkin's First Principle deals with the urge to centralize. His
Second Principle deals with the groupthink approach to decisions, and their avoidance, and indicates the probable origin of
buck passing.

Because of his many distinct characteristics, it is not surprising that the administrator has been described in song as well
as in literature. The most popular appeared during World War
II as a parody of the Air Force song, *Wild Blue Yonder*. The
author, or authors, and the circumstances of its composition are
unknown, but it is as relevant to contemporary bureaucracies
as it was to the military in the 1940s—dealing as it does with
the inertia of the bureaucracy, its insistence upon the preservation of the status quo.

The Chair Corps Song

*Off we go into the file case yonder
Diving deep into the drawer.
There it is, buried away down under,
That damn thing we've been searching for.
Office men guarding the Army's red tape,
We'll be there followed by more.
With dictionary we're stationary,
Nothing can move the Army Chair Corps.*

While the military bureaucracy is celebrated in song and
story, and has been the subject of much searching inquiry, university administrative bureaucracies have also been studied,
though less intensively. When university administration is examined closely, it turns out that the deans are among the most

visible of the university bureaucrats. When the activities of the typical dean are understood clearly, then it is possible to generalize about most academic executives.

To determine the role and scope of the dean's duties, Dean John Randolph Willis made a study of over 100 deans of colleges of arts and sciences. The summary that follows states what the deans themselves said that they did.

What Does the Dean Do?

(1) Have some, but not the final, say on faculty salaries.

(2) Influence decisions on tenure, promotions, and contract renewals, but do not have control.

(3) Have a voice, but not a final one, in hiring and firing faculty.

(4) Do not play any role in student admissions.

(5) Generally, but not always, have a budget which they parcel out to departments.

(6) Have hopes, but no assurances, that they influence policy in their college and university.

(7) Do not control curriculum, or courses or other academic matters.

(8) Do not participate in fund-raising and the suggestions that they should fill most deans with horror.[99]

Willis goes on to report that one dean suggested doubling of all vacation periods. He said, "I work most effectively and at maximum efficiency [doing *what* is unclear] when both the faculty and the students are off the campus." Another confessed that he generally got more work done when he spent less time at the office.

These findings are clearly in harmony with two observations made by Martin.

Martin's Plagiarism of Mark Twain

Deans are mentioned in the Bible.
Blessed are the meek for they shall inherit the earth.[18]

Martin's Plagiarism of H. L. Mencken

Those who can—do. Those who cannot—teach. Those who cannot teach become deans.[18]

It was in the context of these ideas about deans that Father Damian Fandal, formerly Academic Dean at the University of Dallas, formulated his two basic rules for effective administration.

Father Damian Fandal's Rules for Deans

Rule 1—*Hide!!!*

Rule 2—*If they find you, lie!!!*[117]

These rules are very specific methods for decision avoidance and, as such, are applicable generally to all administrators; they need not be so narrowly restricted, just to deans, as Father Fandal suggests.

There is no widespread agreement among recognized hierarchiologists regarding *why* administrators are the way they are. Conventional psychologists have not given the matter the degree of attention it so richly deserves. The most informed supposition, the one most generally accepted by managers anyway, was first formulated by Dr. Howard P. Wile, Executive Director of the Committee on Governmental Relations of the National Association of College and University Business Officers. This is the world famous organization known more familiarly as COGRNACUBO.

Wile on the Administrator

According to Freud, a child's orientation toward the outside world involves a sharp break away from the inwardly directed self-orientation that every child has. He is suddenly required to make adjustments to what is known as the superego.* This comes in the form of injunctions from the outside world to conform to certain rules of behavior—first from his parents, then from his teachers, his age peers, and eventually from almost everyone with whom he has contact. The infant who has had everything his own way is now confronted with weaning, toilet training, and with many other difficult social obligations. This coercion snowballs until the poor thing becomes a pathetic bundle of conflicts, anxieties, and neuroses. This, of course, is ideal preconditioning for a career as an administrator.[62]

This chapter opened with the revelation of the Martin Effect, which stated that executives in educational and governmental hierarchies call themselves administrators. With all that the science of hierarchiology has discovered and publicized to the world about the true character of administrators, one can only be continually surprised that people proudly proclaim themselves one of the breed. Yet they do and Antony Jay finally discovered why.

---

* The best way to think of the superego is to think of it as that part of you that is soluble in alcohol.

Jay's Law of Administrators

Officials in the civil service and the big corporations have hidden behind ... [the title administration] for many years and used "administration" as a mystique to justify drawing leadership-size salaries without exercising the function of leadership.[63]

chapter four

Fuglemanship

As everyone knows, a *fugleman* is a person who stands as an exemplar, an ideal to be emulated. In short, a fugleman is a leader, and *fuglemanship* is the art and science of leadership, which is yet another word for management. There are those who prefer to use the word *gubernator,* which means helmsman, or manager. Unfortunately, this word has been poisoned for most of us through its long association with state governmental hierarchies.

The concept of fuglemanship is pure anathema to the dedicated administrator who was described in Chapter 3. Decision-*making* is organic to leadership and gubernating, while decision *avoidance* is the name of the administrative game. Moreover, as described by the Martin Effect in Chapter 3, management directs and controls change. Such change implies new goals and new directions, and these are dependent upon creative fuglemanship. In contrast, administration resists change and depends upon creative kludgemanship to sustain the status quo. Dr. Michael Polanyi, the Nobel Laureate chemist, made an important point applicable to this difference between manager and administrator. It concerns the assumption of responsibility.

Polanyi's Law of Responsibility

No responsibility is taken where no hazard is to be met, and a hazard is a liability to failure.[64]

Flip Wilson, the television comedian, was less elegant, but conceivably more precise, in his law.

Flip Wilson's Law

You can't expect to hit the jackpot if you don't put a few nickels in the machine.[98]

Administration, as described in Chapter 3, never fails because it assumes no hazards, no responsibility; it only maintains the status quo by enforcement of existing policies and procedures. Management, or leadership, is quite another matter best described through a little poem by Frederick Winsor in *The Space Child's Mother Goose.*

Winsor's Wisdom*

Probable-Possible my black hen
She lays eggs in the Relative When
She doesn't lay eggs in the Positive Now
Because she's unable to postulate how.[65]

It is the role of management to "lay eggs in the Positive Now" by being able to postulate how. Alvin Toffler, writing in his book *Future Shock,* put the managerial role of the fugleman into even more precise terms.

Toffler's Definition of Management

The management of change is the effort to convert certain possibles into probables, in pursuit of agreed on preferables.[66]

The production of change and the ability to control it, require the establishment of new goals, new strategies, new directions. In modern organizations this is a deliberate and calculated process of searching for new ideas, new approaches or new

* Copyright © 1956, 1957, 1958 by Frederick Winsor and Marian Parry; reprinted by permission of Simon & Schuster, Inc.

techniques to "convert certain possibles into probables." In practice it is evident that there are several ways of doing this. Antony Jay, in *Management and Machiavelli,* delineated two extreme alternatives.

Jay on Supply and Demand

There are two ways of looking for a new idea: inward and outward, at what you can make or at what people want, at your supply and their demand.

Obviously, if there is a lack of connection between supply and demand you have got to alter one to fit the other. The trouble is that altering the supply requires a great deal of thought and work and risk . . . a whole lot of . . . complicated and laborious activities. That is why the prospect of altering the demand to fit the supply is so seductive, and a great section of the advertising industry thrives on implying that this can be a solution . . . but there is no evidence that advertising can create a demand that is not there.[66]

Altering the supply requires innovation, perhaps many innovations, in addition to the hard work and risks cited by Jay.

And it is so difficult to secure innovative people. Innovation is generally a highly individualized affair that does not lend itself to the groupthink or committee approach. Terman put the matter into proper perspective.

Terman's Law of Innovation

If you want a track team to win the high jump you find one person who can jump seven feet, not seven people who can each jump one foot.[105]

Because innovative people are few in number, almost impossible to identify, and consequently very hard to find, alteration of supply to meet demand is extremely difficult. In attempting to alter the supply, failure looms as one very probable outcome and, with it, a correspondingly probable major career setback for the responsible executive. It takes a brave manager to choose this path. So, in many cases, product research and even fundamental research are initiated and supported in the hope that the needed innovations will somehow materialize. The desired result is seldom achieved quite this easily because of a phenomenon first described by George Steel and Paul Kucker. They had noted that the electric razor was not invented by a razor blade company; the polaroid process was not developed by Eastman Kodak, the Xerox dry copier was not invented by a maker of ink or spirit duplicators, and so on.

The Crisis We Face*

Picture a man in charge of weapons for a medieval king. If he is scientific minded, he will try to improve his bows and arrows by working on different parts of the product. The searcher may be assigned to study the properties of feathers. He will try to improve the breed of birds, study feather selection and storage, investigate whether they should be trimmed ½- or ¾-inch wide and so on. This man will conduct what many call "scientific research" for years. He may achieve many improvements, giving arrows better stability and accuracy; but what is the chance that such a man will ever invent a gun? If he should hear about one, the chances are he will do his best to point out how unstable and dangerous it is to carry a powder horn, how inaccurate the new guns are, and how many families depend for their livelihood on the chicken feather business.[68]

This deep seated hostility toward the innovation, and the innovator, is a very well known phenomenon. It was described a long time ago by Niccolò Machiavelli, one of the very first hierarchiologists and a fugleman of considerable fame.

Machiavelli on Innovators

It must be remembered that there is nothing more difficult to plan, more doubtful of success, nor more dangerous to manage than the creation of a new system. For the initiator has the enmity of all who would profit by the preservation of the old institutions and merely lukewarm defenders in those who should gain by the new ones.[69]

This has a corollary which was propounded by Dr. Thomas Jones, President of the University of South Carolina.

Tom Jones' First Law

Friends may come and go, but enemies accumulate.[123]

No one should be surprised by the effect described by Machiavelli, because it has its exact analog in the physical sciences in what is known as Le Chatelier's Law.

Le Chatelier's Law

If some stress (such as a change of temperature, pressure, etc.) is brought to bear on a system in equilibrium, the equilibrium is displaced in the direction which tends to undo the effect of the stress.[89]

Every serious student of organizational behavior is familiar with the analog of Le Chatelier's Law in bureaucracies. That is, every attempt to produce a change in a bureaucratic system always creates a counterforce that drives the system back toward the initial condition, thereby preserving the status quo.

The driving force behind the change is usually the manager, and the opposing counterforce clearly originates with the administrators.

There is yet another effect present in all organizations, an effect which inhibits change. The basic phenomenon was first discovered by physical scientists studying the various human senses, such as sight and hearing. Their findings were embodied in the Weber-Fechner Law.

The Weber-Fechner Law

The least change in stimulus necessary to produce a perceptible change in response is proportional to the stimulus already existing.[90]

For example, imagine that you are looking at a black-and-white TV screen in a well-lighted room with the set turned off. The face of the screen appears grayish white from the general room illumination. But, when the set is turned on and the picture appears, some areas of the screen are seemingly black, some are white, and the rest are varying shades of gray. Yet we know that the screen is still illuminated by the same room lighting as before and that there cannot, therefore, really be any black areas—in spite of what we see. Of course, what happens is that certain areas on the screen have been made so bright that the others, by contrast, *seem* black to the eye. As more room lights are directed on the TV screen it becomes necessary to advance the contrast control to maintain the desired degree of apparent blackness. Similarly, to be heard against background noise requires the speaker to raise his voice—so that people end up shouting in one another's ears at cocktail parties. These are both manifestations of the Weber-Fechner Law.

The same effect occurs in organizations. It is often called the *You-Have-To-Run-Faster-To-Stand-Still Syndrome.* In   other words, if an organization is being stimulated somehow to change, through some management action, then to produce another perceptible change it is necessary to produce a force stronger than any already present. As a consequence, it becomes progressively harder and harder to produce changes in an organization. Eventually the level of stimulation is so high that further change is impossible. The organization either dies or is reconstituted through internal revolt or external takeover by an aggressive imperialistic neighbor.

Although opposition to innovation and change is an essential feature of all bureaucracies, it is generally thought to be most apparent in the academic bureaucracies as reported by Dr. Robert L. Saunders, Dean of Engineering at the University of California at Irvine.

Saunders' Laws of Educational Innovation

First Law—*Educational innovation may only be accomplished in the presence of faculty antipathy or euphoria.*

Corollary—*Faculty opposition will stifle innovation and new developments.*

Second Law—*The number of innovative proposals advanced for educational experimentation is inversely proportional to the faculty member's rank.*

Corollary 1—*The most innovative man and the man most receptive to new ideas is the chief campus executive.*

Corollary 2—*Assistant Professors do not wish to change the educational status quo.*[96]

Saunders' conclusions have been criticized by some as possibly being too regionally biased—his "West Coast" provincial chauvinism is well known. Critics cite numerous outstanding cases in which university administrators—presidents, vice-presidents, deans, department chairpersons—are recognizably the Abominable No Men of the academocracy, rather than the faculty as Saunders insists. Actually, both views are now known to be correct. Resistance to change on the campus is so massive, hostility to educational innovation is so intense, that only a close union of faculty and administration could produce such a glacial response to obvious and pressing new needs and demands.

The managerial drive to produce change in the face of solidly entrenched administration has led to some curious semantics. As everyone knows, all physical objects are characterized by a property known as *mass*. Mass is what causes objects to have weight when they are exposed to gravity. In addition, mass in motion can be described in terms of two different factors, inertia and momentum. These two factors are very commonly used to describe the state of a particular bureaucratic organization as well. Martin discovered that, when used in this manner, these terms are interpreted quite differently than is the case in physical descriptions of objects.

The Martin Mass Dichotomy

Momentum is a term used to denote organizational progress.
Inertia is used to denote failure to change.[18]

In physical systems both inertia and momentum are conserved; that is, the total system momentum remains constant, and this is evidenced by the inertia which resists change. Martin has speculated, and there is abundant circumstantial evidence to support him, that, in organizational systems, inertia is conserved but momentum is not.

The techniques of stifling innovation have not been studied in sufficient detail. This is surprising because the process is so widespread. One would think that so common a human practice would have drawn *its* Kinsey, but such is not the case. There is little question but that Parkinson's detailed studies of the Abominable No Man, and the Law of Delay, were important milestones. It is also clear that Rangnekar's conclusions on decision avoidance were closely related to the earliest theory of Change Prevention. However, it was John C. Stedman, in *Education for Innovation,* who first revealed that the prevention of innovation is a highly developed art which, when examined carefully, can often be identified by the following phrases.

Stedman's Killer Phrases

We tried something like that years ago.
That's ridiculous.
That's too radical.
Let's form a committee to consider it.
That's contrary to policy.
Has anyone ever tried it?
It won't work.
That's too obvious to be considered.
That's too superficial.
That's interesting, but we don't have the time or the manpower.
Tell me right now—what's the potential profit in it?
That's not the kind of idea we expect from you.[70]

And then Dr. James Kalan, of the Mathematics Department of the University of Dallas, is justifiably famous for his corollary to Stedman's work.

Kalan's Corollary

If that were possible it would already be in practice.[118]

It is part of modern management practice to be sure that everything that is reduced to practice is covered by a rule. In accordance with Kalan, *everything* that is possible is already in practice and is, correspondingly, covered by a rule. It is obvious then that all situations can be handled by administrators, rather than managers—it is only necessary to find the appropriate rule. This need for rules is the key element in the Bureaucratic Ethic. It was enunciated with great clarity on the night of July 11, 1972, by Congressman James O'Hara, Chairman of the Democratic Party Rules Committee. From the Democratic Presidential Nominating Convention in Miami, on national television, he made the following announcement.

O'Hara's Bureaucratic Ethic

It is more important to have a rule to go by than what the rule actually says.

It is generally understood that hostility to innovation originates in fear, fear that the change from the status quo will create an indeterminate future, one that may be potentially unpleasant, or even disastrous for certain individuals, particularly those in active administration—opposition, that is. As a result, and as we have seen repeatedly, administration is disposed to preserve the status quo.

Conversely, the managerial mandate to create change and to control it requires an open mind to new ideas, a free-wheeling willingness to consider any and all ideas as potentially useful innovations. But then the manager only directs change and allocates organizational resources to make it possible to change. He is not a direct participant in the change process itself. Not surprisingly, then, Weiler found that the managerial propensity to accept change is entirely predictable.

Weiler's Law

Nothing is impossible for the man who doesn't have to do it himself.[71]

An interesting and specific application of Weiler's Law is found in the universities. It will be remembered that Saunders studied innovation on the campus and found that innovativeness increased with movement upward through the hierarchy. This seems obvious now because the likelihood of having to *do* anything at all diminishes rapidly as rank in the academocracy increases. This permits the high-ranking faculty and the academic administrators to speak at great length and with great conviction about the necessity for educational innovation.

One of the reasons there is so little educational reform in the universities is that it should commence with the introductory freshman (I suppose freshperson is more acceptable today) courses. It is quite common to find that these are taught by the most transient people on the campus—either teaching assistants or the nontenured assistant professors. Although these paraprofessional faculty members are frequently enjoined, conned, and hustled by the senior faculty about the importance of these introductory courses, they always remember Waffle's Law.

Waffle's Law

A professor's enthusiasm for teaching the introductory course varies inversely with the likelihood of his having to do it.[97]

This, of course, is an obvious specialization of Weiler's Law.

The execution of the managerial function of fuglemanship requires the assumption of responsibility, the liability to failure, and the power to deploy resources of men, matériel, finance, and organization. The assumption and the exercise of power and authority are the necessary handmaidens for effective management. These tend to be dirty words in contemporary America, usually because Lord Acton's famous law has been accepted as the final and only authoritative statement on the subject.

Lord Acton's Law

Power tends to corrupt and absolute power corrupts absolutely.[72]

Without quarreling about the occasional validity of Acton's Law —after all, one only needs to mention Hitler—it should be observed that the problem he identifies is not the only dimension involved in the exercise of authority, not by any means. There is another risk, and it is generally greater than the one noted by Acton. It is derived from Barbara Tuchman's study of the Chinese Kuomintang. Although her comment was directed specifically to the situation in mainland China, before and during World War II, it is particularly appropriate to contemporary American bureaucracies of all types.

Tuchman's Law

If power corrupts, weakness in the seat of power, with its constant necessity of deals and bribes and compromising arrangements, corrupts even more.[73]

Management weakness, the tendency for the manager to become administrator, is a much greater hazard today to organizational health than is excessive managerial authority. Moreover, it is far more common than the reverse tendency for administrators to become managers. Tuchman's Law reflects the more nearly operational hazard today than does Lord Acton's. Alfred P. Sloan, Jr., also made some very penetrating observations on this same matter during the depths of the Depression in 1931 regarding the situation in General Motors.

Sloan on Management Weakness

First, I think we have lacked ... courage in dealing with weaknesses in personnel. We know weaknesses exist, we tolerate them and finally after tolerating them an abnormal length of time we make the change and then regret that we have not acted before.

Second—We do not get the facts.... We sit around and discuss things without the facts.

Third—I think we become too superficial and we should correct this tendency. Problems are crowding in on us; time is limited....[74]

Management weakness, as described by Sloan, is a very common phenomenon. Everyone confronting difficult problems of personnel weaknesses searches for excuses and reasons to justify inaction—even though it is patently obvious that the results of inaction are worse than any of the consequences of action. Professor L. W. Matsch of the University of Arizona highlighted the issue while agreeing with Sloan.

Matsch's Law

It is better to have a horrible ending than horrors without end.[133]

Much of the cause of the management weakness alluded to by Sloan, as well as that described by Tuchman's Law, results because the executive is buried in paperwork and details. Important issues are obscured while sledgehammer policies are applied to minor or trivial problems. This often leads to policy overkill, a common effect in blunderland. For example, back in 1945 the

U.S. Forest Service mounted a national campaign against forest fires. "Smokey the Bear" was invented, and for the next twenty-seven years he appeared relentlessly on television, telling the public that "Only you can prevent forest fires." Smokey proved to be too successful. As reported in *Time*,[127] in August 1972, ". . . the park areas have been so carefully protected from fire that the pines have become aged and are thus vulnerable [to the mountain pine beetle]." As a result, so many trees are being destroyed by the beetles that the Forest Service is planning to deliberately set fires to "put the forest back into natural balance." The article in *Time* quotes Park Biologist Lloyd Loope as saying, "Smokey the Bear has been lying for years."

The manager faces the daily task of winnowing the wheat of policy matters from the obscuring chaff of detail. In principle, he aims to concentrate upon important policy questions and to refer the routine details to hierarchical subordinates. This process of isolating essential policy matters from the surrounding confusion of misleading detail is an extraordinarily difficult job. However, in recent years it has been simplified considerably through the application of Shimkin's Rule.

Shimkin's Rule

Policy is anything you want to decide yourself, period. Routine details are anything you don't want to be bothered with.[75]

Superficially, of course, the administrator has the same problem as the manager, to winnow the policy matters from the routine chaff. But his aim is to concentrate on the chaff and pass the buck for policy in the direction of least resistance. If he is in an important executive position he quickly becomes a victim of Tuchman's Law and its consequence, best known as Barzun's Law.

Barzun's Law

Abdicating power generates the taste for organized inaction and the pursuit of pseudowork ... to redundant talk, broody sittings of committees, and proliferating plans and reports fore and aft of nonexisting accomplishments.[76]

This kind of activity should not necessarily be condemned out of hand because it can take some of the punishment out of being a manager. And, heaven knows, being a manager is a physically wearing occupation. The annual executive casualty lists make those from Viet Nam look small in comparison. Thus, when we see executives changing from the role of manager to that of administrator, it may very well prove to be nothing more than a reflex action aimed at mere physical survival, rather than a conscious personal goal.

The rapid turnover of fuglemen is unfortunate because leadership implies change, and too frequent change in leadership can result in aimless organizational meandering and zigzagging, with little or no net positive accomplishment, no measurable progress. Antony Jay studied this matter in some detail. His conclusions are given here as Jay's Laws of Leadership.

Jay's Laws of Leadership

First Law—*Changing things is central to leadership, and changing them before anyone else is creativeness.*

Second Law—*To build something that endures it is of the greatest importance to have a long tenure in office, to rule for many years. You can achieve a quick success in a year or two, but nearly all of the great tycoons have continued their building for much longer.*[77]

Any manager serving for a long time, in compliance with Jay's Second Law, sooner or later finds the early blushes of the almost invariable initial success fading into a sallow aftermath of personal frictions, budget reductions, and steady sniping from administrators at the next higher and lower levels. Expenditure reductions must be made, activities must be curtailed, plans must be set aside, acquisitions must be stretched out and inventories reduced. When these unpleasant, but inevitable, conditions prevail, the manager is well advised to be guided by Jay's Law of Economy.

Jay's Law of Economy

Economy does not need an actuary, it needs a visionary.

Corollary—*Trivial and cheese-paring economy drives are one aspect of absence of vision, or failure to transmit it.*[78]

Chapter 3 closed with a statement by Wile, a statement believed to be an accurate description of why the administrator is the way he is. There is no corresponding analysis of the manager. However, it has been discovered that the fugleman, the managerial executive, really has nothing to do. This was proven in *Forbes* Magazine.

Forbes' Famous Law

As everyone knows, an executive has practically nothing to do, except to decide what is to be done; to tell somebody to do it; to listen to reasons why it should not be done, why it should be done by someone else, or why it should be done in a different way; to follow up to see if the thing has been done; to discover that it has been done incorrectly; to point out how it should have been done; to conclude that, as long as it has been done, it might as well be left where it is; to wonder if it is not time to get rid of a person who cannot do a thing right; to reflect that he probably has a wife and a large family, and that certainly any successor would be just as bad, and maybe worse; to consider how much simpler and better the thing would have been done if one had done it oneself in the first place; to reflect sadly that one could have done it in twenty minutes, and as things turned out, one has to spend two days to find out why it has taken three weeks for someone else to do it wrong.[79]

It has been the thesis of this chapter that the manager is a leader, a fugleman, a Willingman, a decision-maker, a person who changes things. He is the exact reverse of the administrator. He is unlikely to be much loved by his hierarchical colleagues at his level, or above or below. But he is armored against the slings and arrows of outraged bureaucrats by a statement which has achieved wide circulation, but which was brought to my attention by Dr. G. M. Nordby of the University of Oklahoma.

Nordby's Nostrum

*Yea, though I walk through the valley
Of the shadow of death
I shall fear no evil,
Because I'm the meanest son-of-a-bitch in the organization.*[80]

The creative practice of fuglemanship invariably generates organizational tensions and many personal frictions. Whether this is good or bad for the organization depends upon who is getting tense, and who is feeling the friction. Abrasiveness is a quality usually attributed to managers and the degree of abrasiveness is usually directly proportional to what he accomplishes. This was first recognized by Fred Bucy, executive vice-president of Texas Instruments, Incorporated.

Bucy's Law

Nothing is ever accomplished by a reasonable man.[93]

There has been a good deal of speculation about this characteristic abrasiveness of managers—is it a natural or a learned characteristic? Are managers natural sons-of-bitches? Or do they become that way because they are managers?

No one is quite sure. But Mike Kingston, writing in *The Dallas Morning News*, reported an event which may shed some light on the matter.

As the Twig Is Bent

There was a mother who was having a hard time getting her son to go to school one morning.

"Nobody likes me at school," said the son, "The teachers don't and the kids don't. The superintendent wants to transfer me, the bus drivers hate me, the school board wants me to drop out and the custodians have it in for me."

"You've got to go," insisted the mother, "You're healthy. You have a lot to learn. You've got something to offer others. You are a leader. Besides, you are forty-nine years old. You're the principal and you've got to go to school."[130]

This brings to mind a statement sent to me by L. W. Matsch[133] which he attributes to Daniel Defoe. It clearly delineates the proper role of the manager in contrast to the administrator.

Defoe's Law

It is better to have a lion at the head of an army of sheep, than a sheep at the head of an army of lions.

It is appropriate to close this chapter with the *one* law that explains more about blunderland than does any other single law or combination—more than Parkinson achieved, more than the

Peter Principle revealed. This discovery is generally attributed to Professor John Imhoff of the University of Arkansas, though he declines credit. Nonetheless, so many engineers associate the law with his name that it seems appropriate to call it Imhoff's Law.

Imhoff's Law

The organization of any bureaucracy is very much like a septic tank. The really big chunks always rise to the top.[108]

chapter five

Academocracy

The four preceding chapters have dealt with the generalized characteristics of bureaucracies and bureaucrats. It was observed that, in the most general terms, a bureaucracy is simply a method of governing or administering a large organization through bureaus or various other subdivisions. It was further noted that bureaucracies are found in government, business, industry, labor, education, medicine, and all other areas which require groups of people to work together.

Once a bureaucracy exists, whether for running a nation, or a large hospital, university, or labor union, the *internal* form of government, the way the bureaucracy is run, can assume a wide variety of forms. For example, it might be:

aristocracy—government by privileged minority
ochlocracy—mob rule
monocracy—government by one man
democracy—government by the people
autocracy—despotic rule by one man
sociocracy—government by society as a whole
theocracy—government by priests
technocracy—government by technicians
adhocracy—government by improvisation

Each of these is a topic of considerable depth within the general boundaries of blunderland, but are beyond the scope of the brief treatment in this book.

This chapter deals with a few limited aspects and manifestations of yet another form of bureaucracy—the educational bureaucracy—or academocracy. In this context it is viewed as an *academ-ocracy.* But, as noted in Chapter 2, the teaching staff tends to view it as an *aca-democracy,* an academic democracy, which is quite another thing. This divergence in viewpoint is at the root of much of the tension that exists between administrators and faculty.

Individual schools, and even universities, have been parts of society for a thousand years, or more in some cases. In the distant past schools and universities were not highly organized, but tended to be loosely knit communities of scholars and students. The bureaucratization of education is a very recent development. It came about largely as a consequence of the Industrial Revolution. With the success of mass production in industry it was only natural to think that the same techniques could be applied in education.

Mass production in industry had clearly proven to be a Good Idea. And Good Ideas achieve lives of their own. This general notion was formalized by Dr. Milton Curry, President of Bishop College.

Curry's Caveat

Any good idea tends to institutionalize itself.[134]

The first step in institutionalizing is organization; and the second step is bureaucratization.

Thus, to achieve educational mass production required educational organization and a hierarchical structure comparable to that found in industry. This analogy was described by Alvin Toffler in his book *Future Shock.*

Toffler on the Educational Bureaucracy

The whole idea of assembling masses of students (raw material) to be processed by teachers (workers) in a centrally located school (factory) was a stroke of industrial genius. The whole administrative hierarchy of education, as it grew up, followed the model of industrial bureaucracy. The very organization of knowledge into permanent disciplines was grounded on industrial assumptions.[136]

In educational organizations the various bureaus, or divisions, are commonly called *departments* with each department representing what is purported to be a major intellectual discipline such as physical education or home economics. In accordance with Toffler's view, it is apparent that educational institutions developed in parallel with their off-campus models in industry and government and evolved into pyramidal hierarchies. As such, the academocracies follow all of the general laws of hierarchiology summarized in the four chapters preceding. Indeed, these chapters included many illustrations drawn from the academic world to illuminate the general laws describing all bureaucracies. Thus, this chapter brings together only those few laws and observations remaining and which seem appropriate only to the academic blunderland.

Academic departments—or divisions, or bureaus, or whatever they may be called in a given school system or university—have become equivalent to the traditional governmental bureaus. They have self-perpetuating lives of their own with all of the instincts of self-protection and aggression associated with Ardrey's Laws of Territorial Imperative.

In the following statement Rosenzweig is discussing the departmental structure within a university. But his words could apply equally well to an analysis of a branch campus in a university system, or the classroom teachers' association (or union) in a public school system.

Rosenzweig's Rubric

On most major campuses the academic department emerged as the spokesman for and protector of its members. It also became, not by coincidence, the entity on campus most capable of producing change, and simultaneously, the one least motivated to do so.[137]

The forces working against genuine innovation, as described in Chapter 4, appear to be more deeply entrenched in education than elsewhere—except in government.

Of course, the educational system and its elements are easy to criticize. One thing that more Americans have in common than almost anything else is their exposure to the educational system. Thus, outside of sex, there are few other subjects on which all Americans feel themselves more expert.

For example, there are those who look at the educational system in relation to the Finagle Theory of Special Relativity described in Chapter 1. In their view society's Desired Results in Fact never equal the Actual Results because

(1) The teachers are introduced into the system merely to apply a series of Finagle Factors taught in teachers' colleges.

(2) Modern educational theories are essentially a series of kludges designed by John Dewey.

Because this leads to a product of a Finagle Factor and a kludge, the result is one monumental SNAFU as predicted by Finagle's Theory.

In actual fact, a good part of education is aimed at overcoming the second version of Rudin's Law—that, if there is a wrong way to do something, most people will do it every time. The effect described by Rudin's Law has plagued contemporary education at all levels, but higher education in particular. Education and its institutions are keystones in support of American society and, in particular, its aspirations for the future. No nation spends as much on, or expects so much of, its educational system. As Jacques Barzun put it:

Barzun's Lament

Education in the United States is a passion and a paradox. Millions want it and commend it, at the same time as they are willing to degrade it by trying to get it free of charge and free of work.[82]

This is certainly clear evidence of Rudin's Law at work.

The cheapening of American education by making it, as Barzun says, "free of charge and free of work" has its roots in the very admirable populist concept of "open admissions." This is another example of the tendency toward counterproductivity that affects all organizations that tamper with Finagle's Second Law—once a job is fouled up, anything done to improve it only makes it worse.

Not enough people remember that education has to do with learning and the mechanism of the learning process is difficult to describe under any circumstances. In particular, certain very essential characteristics are often overlooked by those who believe in "open admission" and "social promotion."

Barzun's Laws of Learning

First Law—*The simple but difficult arts of paying attention, copying accurately, following an argument, detecting an ambiguity or a false inference, testing guesses by summoning up contrary instances, organizing one's time and one's thought for study—all these arts ... cannot be taught in the air but only through the difficulties of a defined subject, [they] cannot be taught in one course or one year, but must be acquired gradually in dozens of connections.*

Second Law—*The analogy to athletics must be pressed until all recognize that in the exercise of Intellect those who lack the muscles,*

*coordination, and will power can claim no place at the training
table, let alone on the playing field.*[83]

It may be that these laws are presently honored more in the
breach than in their observance. They were followed more
closely in earlier times when educational institutions were rather
simple organizations led by towering men of uncommon intellectual foresight. With the rise of the academocracy this is less
likely to be true.

There has been an enormous expansion of the academocracy
that has been continuous since the end of World War II. This is
partly the result of an expanding school-age population, partly a
case of rising social expectations, and partly Parkinson's Law.
However, with the current decline in birth rate and elementary
school–age population, and with the increasing public disfavor
regarding the value of a college education, expansion can continue only if the Parkinsonian pressure is dominant. Although
the answer is not perfectly clear, it seems that many school dis-
tricts and university systems are still expanding their physical
facilities.

Although it is a rather overly simplistic view, it is convenient
to consider any educational system as a troika, consisting of
faculty, students, and the administration. Each of these is discussed very briefly in this chapter, but only in the special context
of colleges and universities.

The situation in higher education provides excellent examples
of both Parkinson's Law and Bunk Carter's Law. Because all
bureaucrats play the same games according to the same rules,
one can scarcely fault the faculty for following suit. Hacker, with
a fine degree of insensitivity to faculty sensibilities made the
following points.

Hacker on the Professoriate

Point 1—*In 1900, forty-one out of every 100,000 employed Americans were college or university professors. By 1964, more than 700 out of every 100,000 had faculty positions.*

Point 2—*The idea that any profession can undergo so great a numerical expansion and still maintain the quality it hitherto had is one of the major illusions of democracies. Such sophistry can, of course, raise the esteem of those recently admitted to professional standing. It is not the first time that reality has been redefined in order to encourage self-congratulation.*

Point 3—*In the light of the expanded academic population, much of contemporary scholarship may best be viewed as environmental adaptations devised to provide honorable occupations for Americans of middling intelligence.*[138]

Hacker's First and Second Points taken together are clearcut manifestations of Parkinson's First Law—that work expands to fill the time available. The Second Point alone is precise evidence that the academocracy responds to Bunk Carter's Law—that, at any given time, there are more important people than there are important jobs. Hacker's Third Point would also appear to arise from Bunk Carter's Law.

Point 3 has some significant consequences of sufficient subtlety that they could be overlooked. The chain of logic might proceed as follows:

(1) Because of Parkinson's First Law, it is necessary that school systems and universities expand continuously.

(2) As a consequence, and also because of Bunk Carter's Law, it is necessary that these systems and universities be staffed with a continuously increasing number of professors.

(3) In accordance with Corollary 2 of Parkinson's First Law

—that officials (professors) make work for each other—
the ever-increasing faculty turns actively to ever-increasing
scholarly research and publication.

(4) This huge, unremitting outpouring of information creates
more confusion than communication in accordance with
Everitt's Corollary to Shannon's Law.

But the events set up by the expansion of the system do not
stop at this point. Because there are large numbers of professors
and teachers in a multitude of minute specialties, they organize
themselves into various professional societies. Each such society
requires a president, assorted other officers, editors, annual meetings, committee chairmen, awards, and so on—thereby creating
more opportunities for affirmative action plans in response to
Bunk Carter's Law.

A significant portion of the scholarly efforts of the professoriate
is devoted to textbook writing. This being a human enterprise, it
is governed by the laws compiled in Chapter 1, and most specifically, by Murphy's Law.

Murphy's Laws of College Publishing
Applications to Publishers

First Law—*Availability of manuscripts in a given subject area is
inversely proportional to the need for books in that area.*

Second Law—*A manuscript for a market in which no textbooks
currently exist will be proceeded two weeks after contracting by an
announcement of an identical book by your closest competitor.*

Applications to Teachers

First Law—*Teacher's guides and answer books will not be ob-
tainable until after you have taught from the text at least once and
developed your own answers.*

Second Law—*The number of luncheon invitations from publisher representatives is directly proportional to the number of students in your classes.*

Applications to Students

First Law—*If your teacher requires that you purchase n books to study for an examination, there will be n − 1 books in stock at the bookstore.*[135]

With so many university faculty on the scene, they have attracted the attention of some who have tried to describe why academocrats are the way they are. For example, Clark Kerr was mentioned in Chapter 3 in connection with his specialization of Hildebrand's Law. However, Kerr also investigated the massive resistance to change so characteristic of the academocracy. This led to his Second Law, which is very widely known and quoted because it encapsulates within a few words the essential explanation of so much that occurs within the academocracy.

Kerr's Second Law

In his dealings on the campus, a faculty member is an ultra-conservative, leaning slightly to the right of Herbert Hoover; in his dealings off campus with the general public his position is as a raging liberal far to the left of Karl Marx.[95]

Martin is responsible for a popular simplification of Kerr's Law.

The Kerr-Martin Law

In dealing with their own problems, faculty members are the world's most extreme conservatives. In dealing with other people's problems they are the world's most extreme liberals.[18]

After being attracted initially by Kerr's work, Martin branched off into other studies of the academic bureaucracy. Although now a hierarchiologist of some note, Martin was originally a statustician, a follower of Vance Packard who founded the science of statustistics in his book *The Status Seekers*. As everyone knows, the laws of statustistics are determined *a priori*, heuristically, and intuitively. As a result, Martin's Laws of Academic Status are intuitively obvious to all thoughtful observers of academocracy.

Martin's Laws of Academic Status

First Law—*A faculty member's true national academic stature as a scholar tends to be inversely proportional to the degree of his involvement in the affairs of the American Association of University Professors.*

Second Law—*A faculty member's professional productivity tends to be inversely proportional to his wife's involvement in the Faculty Women's Club.*

Third Law—*Departmental prestige on campus is directly proportional to its physical distance from the Plants and Grounds Building.*

Corollary—*Buildings in the College of Engineering are always located immediately adjacent to the power plant.*[18]

The students form the second component of the university troika as noted earlier. Much has been said about college students in recent years, and they probably deserved every bit of it. However, the reader surely has his own well-established opinions or prejudices. Thus, instead of once again covering familiar ground, it seems more constructive to take a slightly different viewpoint.

Under current circumstances in which over half of the nation's high-school graduates go to college, it is natural to wonder what happens to them when they get there. Moreover, for many years a college diploma has been considered to be the necessary certificate for entry into an increasing proportion of the available jobs. The validity of this certification process has rarely been questioned in print. As a career academocrat I am convinced that higher education is a Good Thing, both for the soul and for job preparation. This is a visceral feeling appropriate to a true contemporary intellectual.

It is no longer necessary to depend upon intuition. Both of these matters, what happens to the college student and the need for certification, have been analyzed in research completed only very recently by Grant. His work definitely brings these issues into clearer perspective.

Grant's Research Results

Research showed that only one of every four students gets a degree; that there are twice as many suicides among college students as among the general population; that college students have fifty percent more mental and emotional problems than the general public; and that there is little or no correlation between grades in college and later success. In addition ... if a student invested the equivalent of the costs of four years of college, he would have larger lifetime earnings than if he attended college.

Therefore ... by attending college, a young person has a better chance of:

Becoming a dropout;
Going crazy;
Killing himself;
Learning irrelevant things;
Losing money.[139]

While I do not share Grant's opinion, students of college enrollment trends are beginning to believe that it is gaining a wider public acceptance.

Administrators form the third and final element of the university troika. One can suggest some of the structure in the pecking order among the academocrats by recounting a very brief episode that occurred recently on my campus. The president of the Rotary Club called the president of the university requesting a speaker for an upcoming meeting. He stressed the high quality of the club membership repeatedly, making it clear that he wanted one of the real top members of the university administration. He closed by saying, "So, Mr. President, we would hope that you would send us a speaker whose rank is no lower than dean." The president of the university responded, "Sir, on this campus there isn't anyone lower than a dean."

One point is often overlooked in the analysis of the academocracy, and it is crucially important. Just because universities are bureaucratized so that they seem indistinguishable from government, business, or the military does not mean that the appearance is correct. The distinction lies in the fact that universities also have a legislature, either a faculty senate or a faculty-student council, of some sort. This legislature is composed of members of the bureaucracy itself and this makes the academocracy a vastly different organization from those in business, industry, or government.

For example, in the military, in industry, in business or labor, or in big medicine, there is no legislature at all. In government the legislature is *separate* from the bureaucracy, which is usually associated with the executive branch. This overlap of bureaucrat and legislator is an additional complexity of substantial magnitude that makes academic administration infinitely more complex than administration in any other bureaucracy—and it makes management virtually impossible.

In any event, when reading criticism of university administration, it is well to keep the foregoing in mind. Rosenzweig is less charitable in his view.

Rosenzweig on University Administrators

The deficiencies that the university administrators bring to the task of governing are largely self-made. Chief among them is an underlying feeling that it is somehow wrong to try to govern an educational institution, that the very processes of governing, e.g., the act of leading, will destroy the values distinctive to universities. In universities the classic democratic problem of the strong executive versus the strong legislature has been answered by a resolve to have neither. Consequently, the typical university administration is part custodial and part promotional. Incredibly, when students say that the administrative function is to keep the place reasonably clean and replace burned-out light bulbs, many administrators silently nod their heads.[140]

Epilogue

According to the dictionary, the purpose of an epilogue is to provide a closing section which supplies further comment, interpretation, or information. Such attempts commonly fall victim to Finagle's Second Law—once a job is fouled up, anything done to improve it only makes it worse. This effort is unlikely to be an exception. We already know that botchulism is extremely contagious; no one is really immune.

It has been the purpose of this book, as stated originally in the Preface, to bring together in one place, in related sequences, all of the laws of executive and organizational behavior that can be found. As is probably evident, this effort has been only partly successful. In accordance with the Backlog Syndrome, this fact leaves the author secure in the knowledge that because his work is still undone he is still needed and his continuing importance is necessarily assured.

The organization of the book is reasonably self-evident with the various chapters providing the threads of relatedness for the many laws, principles, observations, axioms, and rubrics that have been compiled. Thus:

Chapter 1—Summarizes laws describing how things go wrong, showing that human intervention in the form of creative and enlightened kludgemanship is the invariable and principal causative agent.

Chapter 2—Proves that human intervention in events is an intentional and highly organized process achieved through the instrumentality of the hierarchical bureaucracy. While the importance of Parkinson's Laws and the Peter Principle are noted, it is generally concluded that the most significant contribution is that due to Bunk Carter—that at any given time there are more important people in the world than important jobs to contain them.

Chapter 3—The world of the bureaucracy, blunderland to be precise, is shown to be inhabited by only two tribes of people, administrators and managers. The chapter presents an extensive compilation of laws describing the characteristics and behavior of administrators. Parkinson's description of the Abominable No Man is the pivotal point in this presentation, particularly when viewed in parallel with the concepts of decidophobia and decision avoidance.

Chapter 4—Provides a comprehensive anthology of the laws of managerial behavior. These ride primarily upon two general concepts. The first is Weiler's Law that nothing is impossible for the man who doesn't have to do it himself. The second is Bucy's Law that nothing is ever accomplished by a reasonable man.

Chapter 5—Serves to illustrate how the general laws of the first four chapters can be applied to a special type of bureaucracy, the academic blunderland.

The sudden ending of the book after Chapter 5 leaves me with a gnawing sense of incompletion, a feeling that the brave goal stated in the Preface has not been achieved. There is still so much yet to be done. There are so many specialized bureaucracies in the labor unions, in both amateur and professional athletics, in the military, in advertising, in book publishing, in organized medicine—everywhere you look. And each has its own special laws, axioms, theorems, and principles simply waiting to be collected. The subject calls for an organized, team effort directed by some large commercial think-tank with the results to be published by the Encyclopedia Britannica. This general result should have been anticipated from Vail's Second Axiom that the percentage of work that remains uncompleted is invariant. In any event, it did lead to an important corollary.

Martin's Corollary to Vail's Second Axiom

The number of laws of executive and organizational behavior to be collected increases in proportion to the number already collected.[18]

Moreover, according to Shannon's Law, what is actually happening is less important than what appears to be happening. Thus, Alvin Toffler in his book *Future Shock* concludes that there really isn't any problem anyway because he feels that the bureaucracies are dying, being replaced by what he calls adhocracies. By this he means that organizational forms are constantly shifting and changing so that unique, one-of-a-kind organizational formats evolve to attack particular problems. Once those problems are solved the organizations fade away to be replaced by new and different structures designed to respond to wholly new problems. This is what he calls adhocracy, a sort of management by improvisation.

Toffler is wrong. Apparently he detects only the *appearance* of organizational change and mistakes this for fundamental change. The truth is that a bureaucracy is similar to an influenza virus; it constantly mutates into new and ever more virulent forms, but it never becomes anything other than a bureaucracy. Toffler seems to have mistaken these mutations for basic changes and then foresees the decline of bureaucracy. But then, he is not familiar with Shannon's Law given earlier. Moreover, the bureaucratic virus, like its influenza counterpart, is extremely difficult to treat with any sort of vaccine, largely because vaccines are effective only against specific and individual mutations. While there is no "magic bullet" available in the war against bureaucracy, understanding is the next best weapon and that has been the purpose of this book.

Through this book I have tried to show that almost every effort of almost every bureaucrat in almost every bureaucracy is counterproductive, nearly always producing results contrary to those predicted and planned, yielding kludges and SNAFUS one after another. So, in contemporary vernacular, when it comes to bureaucracy, nothing there is where it's at. And that is malice in blunderland.

References and Sources

1. From "The Amateur Scientist," *Scientific American,* April 1956, p. 166; copyright © 1956 by Scientific American, Inc. All rights reserved. With permission.

2. Jim Wright, "On Second Thought," *The Dallas Morning News,* September 9, 1969; with permission of the author.

3. Quoted by Brooks Atkinson.

4. Quoted by Robert L. Bates in the "Geologic Column," *GeoTimes,* July–August 1968; with permission of the author and the editor.

5. Attributed to Thoreau by William H. Whyte, Jr., *The Organization Man,* Simon & Schuster, Inc., New York. Copyright © 1956 by William H. Whyte, Jr.

6. Edmund C. Berkeley, *Computers and Automation,* September 1969, v. 18, n. 10, p. 20; reprinted with permission of the editor.

7. Francis P. Chisholm, *The Chisholm Effect,* originally published in *motive magazine,* P.O. Box 871, Nashville, Tenn.; with the permission of the editor.

8. Eric Sevareid, *CBS News,* December 29, 1970.

9. Attributed to *The Daily Independent* in *Weight Watchers Magazine,* January 1971, p. 68; reprinted with permission from *Weight Watchers Magazine.*

10. Adapted from *African Genesis,* by Robert Ardrey; copyright © 1961 by Literat S.A.; reprinted by permission of Atheneum Publishers.

11. Excerpts from pp. 68, 69, 70 from *Management and Machiavelli* by Antony Jay. Copyright © 1967 by Antony Jay. Reprinted by permission of Holt, Rinehart and Winston, Inc.

12. Alfred P. Sloan, Jr., *My Years with General Motors,* MacFadden-Bartell Corp., N.Y., 1965, p. 48; reprinted with permission of Harold Matson, Inc., N.Y. Copyright © 1963 by Alfred P. Sloan, Jr.

13. Charles A. Reich, *The Greening of America*, originally published in *The New Yorker*, September 26, 1970, p. 54: subsequently published in book form by Random House, Inc., with permission of *The New Yorker* and Random House, Inc. Copyright © 1970 by Charles A. Reich.

14. Ward Just, "Soldiers—Part II," *The Atlantic Monthly*, November 1970, pp. 67–68, quoting Fitzhugh on the Pentagon; with permission of the author.

15. Ortega y Gasset, *Man and People*, copyright © 1957 by W. W. Norton & Co., Inc., N.Y., p. 140; reprinted with permission of the publisher.

16. John Gregory Dunne, "To Die Standing—Cesar Chavez and the Chicanos," *The Atlantic Monthly*, June 1971, p. 40; reprinted with the permission of International Famous Agency.

17. Anonymous.

18. Thomas L. Martin, Jr., Dean, Institute of Technology, Southern Methodist University, Dallas, Texas.

19. Andrew Hacker, *The End of the American Era*, Atheneum, N.Y., 1970, p. 143; reprinted with permission of the publisher. Copyright © 1968, 1970 by Andrew Hacker.

20. Antony Jay (ref. 11), *op. cit.*, p. 70; with permission of the publisher.

21. Andrew Hacker (ref. 19), *op. cit.*, p. 17; reprinted with permission of the publisher.

22. Charles R. Vail, Vice-President, Southern Methodist University; published with his permission.

23. C. Northcote Parkinson, *Parkinson's Law*, Houghton-Mifflin Co., Boston, 1957; reprinted with permission of the publisher. Copyright © 1957 by C. Northcote Parkinson.

24. C. Northcote Parkinson, *The Law and the Profits*, Houghton-Mifflin Co., Boston, 1960; reprinted with permission of the publisher. Copyright © 1960 by C. Northcote Parkinson.

25. Parkinson (ref. 23), *op. cit.*; reprinted with permission of the publisher.

26. Dr. Laurence J. Peter and Raymond Hull, *The Peter Principle: Why Things Go Wrong*, William Morrow & Company, Inc., New York, 1969. Copyright © 1969 by William Morrow & Company, Inc.

27. *Ibid.*, p. 25.

28. *Ibid.*, p. 27.

29. *Ibid.*, p. 27.

30. *Ibid.*, p. 27.

31. *Ibid.*, p. 45.

32. *Ibid.*, p. 63.

33. *Ibid.*, p. 54.

34. *Ibid.*, p. 56.

35. *Ibid.*, p. 101.

36. *Ibid.*, p. 107.

37. *Ibid.*, p. 157.

38. *Ibid.*, p. 135.

39. Arthur J. Riggs, "Parkinson's Law, the Peter Principle and the Riggs Hypothesis—A Synthesis," *Michigan Business Review*, March 1971, v. 13, n. 2, pp. 23–25; reprinted with permission.

40. William Wilkerson, *The Comanche Chief* (Texas), quoted by Mike Kingston in *The Dallas Morning News*, October 5, 1970, on the editorial page; reprinted with permission.

41. W. C. Bennett, Trinity Avenue Presbyterian Church, Durham, N.C., supplied by C. R. Vail; reprinted with permission of Dr. Bennett.

42. Richard H. Brien, "The Managerialization of Higher Education," *Educational Record*, Summer 1970, v. 51, n. 3, p. 274; reprinted with permission of The American Council on Education, Washington, D.C.

43. Charles A. Reich (ref. 13), *op. cit.,* p. 50.

44. Attributed to Sam Rayburn in "Report from Washington," *The Atlantic Monthly,* December 1970, p. 17; reprinted with permission.

45. James Boren, "Maximizing NATAPROBU," President NATAPROBU (National Association of Professional Bureaucrats), in *Time,* November 23, 1970, p. 44; reprinted by permission from *Time, the Weekly Newsmagazine;* copyright © Time, Inc., 1970.

46. Jerome Cohen, Harvard Law Professor, quoted in *Time,* June 7, 1971, p. 24: "Tense Triangle: What to Do about Taiwan"; reprinted by permission from *Time, the Weekly Newsmagazine;* copyright © Time, Inc., 1971.

47. Source unknown.

48. C. Northcote Parkinson, *The Law of Delay,* Houghton-Mifflin Co., Boston, 1970, pp. 116–117; reprinted with permission of the publisher. Copyright © 1970 by C. Northcote Parkinson.

49. Sharu S. Rangnekar, *The Art of Avoiding Decisions,* mimeograph, 3 pp., date unknown; efforts to locate the author, or any other details, have failed; believed to be from the University of Michigan, circa 1970.

50. Herbert V. Prochnow. *A Dictionary of Wit, Wisdom, and Satire,* copyright © 1962 by Herbert V. Prochnow and Herbert V. Prochnow, Jr., Harper & Row, N.Y., 1962, with permission.

51. Rangnekar (ref. 49), *op. cit.*

52. C. Northcote Parkinson (ref. 23), *op. cit.,* pp. 50, 62; reprinted with permission of the publisher.

53. *Ibid.,* reprinted with permission of the publisher.

54. Source unknown.

55. E. R. Hendrickson, president, Environmental Engineering, Inc., Gainesville, Florida; published with his permission.

56. William H. Whyte, Jr. (ref. 5), *op. cit.,* pp. 57–58, reprinted with permission.

57. Excerpts from pp. 69, 77, 89, 95, 113–114 in *The House of Intellect*. Copyright © 1959 by Jacques Barzun. By permission of Harper & Row, Publishers, Inc.

58. Martin (ref. 18).

59. Rangnekar (ref. 49).

60. Parkinson (ref. 48), *op. cit.*, p. 119; reprinted with permission of the publisher.

61. Michael B. Shimkin, "Principles of Research Administration," in *Stress Analysis of a Strapless Evening Gown*, ed. by Robert A. Baker, Prentice-Hall, Inc., 1963, pp. 161–169. Reprinted with permission of Michael B. Shimkin.

62. Howard P. Wile, Executive Director, Committee on Governmental Relations, National Association of College and University Business Officers, Washington, D.C.; reprinted with his permission.

63. Jay (ref. 11), *op. cit.*, p. 81; reprinted with permission of the publisher.

64. Michael Polanyi, *The Study of Man*, University of Chicago Press, Chicago, 1958, p. 67; with permission of the publisher. Copyright 1959 by the University College of North Staffordshire.

65. Frederick Winsor and Marian Parry, *The Space Child's Mother Goose*, verse no. 1. Copyright © 1956, 1957, 1958 by Frederick Winsor and Marian Parry. Reprinted by permission of Simon & Schuster, Inc.

66. Alvin Toffler, *Future Shock*, Random House, N.Y., 1970, p. 407; reprinted with permission of the publisher. Copyright © 1970 by Alvin Toffler.

67. Jay (ref. 11), *op. cit.*, pp. 92–94; reprinted with permission of the publisher.

68. From *The Crisis We Face*, by George Steel and Paul Kucker, copyright © 1960 by McGraw-Hill Book Company, N.Y., pp. 35–36; used with permission of McGraw-Hill Book Company.

69. From *The Prince*, by Niccolò Machiavelli, trans. and edited by Thomas G. Bergin; copyright © 1947, Crofts Classics. By permission of Appleton-Century-Crofts, Educational Division, Meredith Corp., p. 15.

70. John C. Stedman, "Engineering and the Many Cultures," in *Education for Innovation*, ed. Daniel V. DeSimone, Pergamon Press, Inc., N.Y., 1968, chap. 3, p. 40; with permission. Copyright © 1968 by Pergamon Press, Inc.

71. Movie editor of *The New York Times*, quoted by Robert L. Bates in the "Geologic Column," *GeoTimes*, July–August 1968; with permission of the author and publisher.

72. Lord Acton in a letter to Creighton on April 5, 1887.

73. Barbara Tuchman, "If Asia Were Clay in the Hands of the West—The Stilwell Mission to China, 1942–44," *The Atlantic Monthly*, September 1970, p. 80; reprinted with permission of Russel & Volkening, Inc.

74. Sloan (ref. 12), *op. cit.*, p. 174, addressing the Operations Committee of General Motors on January 9, 1931.

75. Shimkin (ref. 61), *op. cit.*; reprinted with permission.

76. Barzun (ref. 57), *op. cit.*, p. 77.

77. Jay (ref. 11), *op. cit.*, pp. 83, 135; reprinted with permission of the publisher.

78. *Ibid.*, p. 125; reprinted with permission of the publisher.

79. Attributed to J. L. McCafferty by Malcolm S. Forbes, Editor-in-Chief, *Forbes Magazine*, November 1, 1970, p. 16, with permission.

80. Gene M. Nordby, Vice-President for Finance, University of Oklahoma, Norman; used with his permission.

81. W. L. Everitt, Dean Emeritus, College of Engineering, University of Illinois, Urbana; in a personal letter dated May 2, 1972; reprinted with his permission.

82. Barzun (ref. 57), *op. cit.*, p. 89.

83. *Ibid.*, pp. 113–114, 95.

84. Russell Baker, quoted in *Time*, January 17, 1972, p. 63; statement reprinted by permission from TIME, the Weekly Newsmagazine. Copyright © Time Inc.

85. Source unknown.

86. Adapted from *African Genesis*, by Robert Ardrey, pp. 77–78; copyright © 1961 by Literat S.A.; reprinted by permission of Atheneum Publishers.

87. *Ibid.*, p. 173; reprinted by permission of Atheneum Publishers.

88. Adapted from *The Territorial Imperative* by Robert Ardrey, p. 162; copyright © 1966 by Robert Ardrey. Reprinted by permission of Atheneum Publishers.

89. C. F. Hix, Jr., and R. P. Alley, *Physical Laws and Effects*, John Wiley & Sons, Inc., N.Y., 1958, p. 128; reprinted with permission of the authors. Copyright © 1958 by General Electric Co.

90. *Ibid.*, p. 225; reprinted with permission of the authors.

91. *Time*, March 6, 1972, p. 52; "Books: The Difference," a review of a then-forthcoming book *Beyond Guilt and Justice* by Walter Kaufman; reprinted by permission from *Time, the Weekly Newsmagazine*; copyright © Time, Inc.

92. R. E. Woolsey, *Management Science Today—Or, Does an Education in Checkers Really Prepare One for a Life of Chess*, p. 3 of a paper given at the S.M.U. Institute of Technology around January 1972.

93. Fred Bucy, Executive Vice-President, Texas Instruments, Incorporated, Dallas, Texas; with permission.

94. Joel Hildebrand, Professor of Chemistry, the University of California at Berkeley; supplied by Robert M. Saunders (ref. 96).

95. Clark Kerr, formerly Chancellor of the University of California; supplied by Robert M. Saunders (ref. 96).

96. Robert M. Saunders, Dean, College of Engineering, University of California at Irvine; with permission.

97. Bates (ref. 71), *op. cit.*; reprinted with permission of the author and editor.

98. Flip Wilson on his television show, October 28, 1971.

99. Adapted from the October 1970 issue of *College Management* Magazine from the article "What Does the Dean Do?" by Dean John Randolph Willis, pp. 26–27. This article is copyrighted © 1970 by CCM Professional Magazines, Inc. All rights reserved.

100. Hix and Alley (ref. 89), *op. cit.*, p. 269; reprinted with permission of the authors.

101. George S. Caldwell, *Good Old Harry—The Wit and Wisdom of Harry S. Truman*, Hawthorne Books, Inc., N.Y., 1966, p. 18; reprinted with permission of the publisher. Copyright © 1966 by Hawthorne Books, Inc.

102. Adapted from *The Territorial Imperative* by Robert Ardrey, p. 167; copyright © 1966 by Robert Ardrey. Reprinted by permission of Atheneum Publishers.

103. *Ibid.*, p. 173; reprinted by permission of Atheneum Publishers.

104. *Ibid.*, pp. 183–184, 186; reprinted by permission of Atheneum Publishers.

105. Frederick E. Terman, Provost Emeritus, Stanford University, Stanford, Cal.; published with his permission.

106. Albert Bowker, Chancellor, City University of New York; supplied by F. E. Terman and printed with his permission.

107. Dan Greenburg and Marcia Jacobs, *How to Make Yourself Miserable*, Random House, N.Y., 1966, p. 12; copyright © 1966 by Dan Greenburg. Reprinted by permission of the publisher.

108. Professor John Imhoff, Head of the Department of Industrial Engineering, University of Arkansas, Fayetteville. A distant cousin, Karl Imhoff, invented the Imhoff Septic Tank of international fame.

109. Prochnow (ref. 50), *op. cit.*

110. From *Engineersmanship: A Philosophy of Design,* by Lee Harrisberger, p. 112; copyright © 1966 by Wadsworth Publishing Co., Inc. Reprinted by permission of the publisher, Brooks/Cole Publ. Co., Monterey, Cal.

111. Jackson W. Granholm, "How to Design a Kludge," *Datamation,* February 1962. Reprinted with permission of *Datamation* ®. Copyright 1962, F. D. Thompson Publications, Inc.

112. Frank M. Wozencraft, Baker and Botts, One Shell Plaza, Houston, Texas; published with his permission.

113. Paul Crume, "Big D," *The Dallas Morning News,* January 21, 1972, p. 1; reprinted with permission.

114. Michael O'Hagan, Dean, Academic Affairs, University of Dallas, Dallas, Texas; published with his permission.

115. Joe Dobbins (now deceased), formerly electronics model shop foreman, Texas Instruments, Incorporated, Dallas, Texas; supplied by Michael O'Hagan.

116. Len Walsh, *Read Japanese Today,* Chas. E. Tuttle Co., publishers, Rutland, Vt. and Tokyo, Japan, 1969, p. 138; with permission.

117. Father Damian C. Fandal O.P., Former Dean of Academic Affairs, University of Dallas, Dallas, Texas; published with his permission.

118. James E. Kalan, Assistant Professor of Mathematics, University of Dallas, Dallas, Texas; published with his permission.

119. Earl R. Gomersall, "The Backlog Syndrome," *Harvard Business Review,* September 1964, pp. 105–115.

120. "Industry at Work," *Oilways,* n. 2, 1972, pp. 16–17; Humble Oil & Refining Co., Houston, Texas; with permission.

121. Edmund C. Berkeley, editor, *Computers and Automation,* in a personal letter dated July 10, 1972; published with his permission.

122. Supplied by G. M. Nordby (ref. 80); attributed to Colonel Gus Peters in Viet Nam, in August 1968; *The Chelsea,* Sydney, Australia.

123. Thomas Jones, President, the University of South Carolina, "Confronting the Financial Crisis," a speech given in Washington, D.C. Supplied by G. M. Nordby (ref. 80).

124. *The Dallas Morning News*, August 2, 1972, p. 3D, byline Terry Kliewer.

125. Edmund C. Berkeley, *The C & A Notebook on Common Sense, Elementary and Advanced*, v. 1, n. 20, 1971, "How to Be Silly"; reprinted with permission.

126. Reprinted by permission from TIME, The Weekly Newsmagazine, August 21, 1972, "People," p. 27. Copyright © Time Inc.

127. Reprinted by permission from TIME, The Weekly Newsmagazine, August 7, 1972, "The Fires Next Time." Copyright © Time Inc.

128. William V. Shannon, "The Amazing Myth of George McGovern," *The Dallas Morning News*, July 2, 1972, p. 28A, Focus.

129. As quoted in *Reader's Digest*, September 1972, from *Sports Illustrated*, June 5, 1972. © 1972 Time Inc.

130. Mike Kingston, *The Dallas Morning News*, "The Texas Press," January 8, 1973; attributed to the *Nacogdoches Daily Sentinel*; with permission.

131. Supplied by Jack P. Holman, Head, Department of Civil and Mechanical Engineering, Southern Methodist University, Dallas, Texas; with permission.

132. Supplied by Mrs. J. P. Holman. Used with her permission.

133. Leander W. Matsch, Professor Emeritus of Electrical Engineering, the University of Arizona, Tucson, Arizona. Printed with his permission.

134. Milton Curry, President of Bishop College, February 8, 1973, at a meeting of the ad hoc Committee on the Future of Goals for Dallas. Printed with his permission.

135. "Applications of Murphy's Law to College Publishing," by Stephen Mitchell, *Computer Science News*, December 1972, Science Research Associates, Palo Alto, Cal.

136. Toffler, *op. cit.*, p. 355; with permission.

137. Robert M. Rosenzweig, "Who Wants to Govern the University?," *Educational Record*, Summer 1970, v. 51, n. 3, p. 268; with permission.

138. Hacker, *op. cit.*, p. 196, 197, 207.

139. *The Chronicle of Higher Education*, April 21, 1969; with permission.

140. Rosenzweig, *op. cit.*, p. 270.

141. A contribution of Hélène H. Martin.

Index